Lost and Found

COOKE BOYD

NEWMAN SPRINGS PUBLISHING
320 Broad Street
Red Bank, NJ 07701

First originally published by Newman Springs Publishing 2021

ISBN 978-1-63881-046-9 (Paperback)
ISBN 978-1-63881-047-6 (Digital)

Printed in the United States of America

To my parents who instilled in me the gift of imagination, broad thinking, the value of dreams, and an appreciation for nature.

To my greatest treasures, my wonderful children and my two beautiful grandkids.

This story would never have come about without the guidance of Sydney Clark, my amazing English teacher in boarding school. Syd taught me the beauty of words and reading. He taught me to write and to express myself, so I think Syd would enjoy the journey.

To my wonderful editor Lee Dunbar for her belief in my ability to write and for her patience in editing my story.

Lastly, to my Stevie, my beautiful wife, who has always been there through good times and bad, bless you.

CHAPTER 1

October 11, 2018

Annie Rogers stood on a small precipice high up in Glacier Park. Beyond that point, there was nothing to prevent her from plunging to her death. A brisk wind began to push her closer to ending it all. You see, the love of her life, Tom, had taken a solo hike in the park and had not returned. It had been three days since a search party was deployed, but there was no sign of her man. The presumption was that he either fell to his death or attacked by a grizzly bear or was taken over by hyperthermia as the night temps were in the twenties. For the last couple of days, Annie had been pacing around her house, cell phone in hand, mumbling that she couldn't go on; there was no point—she knew what she had to do.

Six years before, she left her home in Maine after her daughters divorced her for what they thought she had done to their father. Somehow, he had convinced them that their mother was abusive and had cheated on him; none of that was true—quite the opposite. Now with Tom, a man she only met recently but loved deeply, missing and presumed dead, she wondered if there was a reason to continue living; to her, there wasn't.

> *You can get over the loss of a watch or a wallet, but*
> *you can never get over the loss of someone you love.*

CHAPTER 2

March 2, 2018

Annie was wielding her cart through the aisles of the little grocery store in her town of Hungry Horse, Montana. As she rounded the corner to get some cereal, she crashed into another cart coming the other way.

"Are you okay?" asked the startled stranger.

"Yes, thank you, are you?" Annie answered and asked, not taking her eyes off the most gorgeous man she had ever seen. Noticing he had a canister of oatmeal in his cart, she asked where he had found the exact cereal she had been looking for. Annie knew, of course, where to find the cereal, as she had shopped in the store for many years, but she wanted to keep the conversation going a bit longer. Glancing down at his left hand, she saw, to her delight, there was no wedding ring on his finger.

"I'm glad I didn't hurt you," the very handsome tall man said.

After telling Annie where the cereal was, they bid each other a good day; Annie was wondering if she would ever see him again, or was he just passing through? She figured if he did live in the area, they would cross paths at some point as her little town was just that, little; everyone knew everyone.

The next day, as Annie was standing in line at the local coffee shop, the Crabby Moose, she saw that beautiful man walk through the door; her knees instantly buckled. Normally she would get her coffee and leave, but wanting to strike up a longer conversation than the day before, she took a seat near the front door, hoping he would stop and say hello. Annie saw him make his purchase, and then he headed towards her table, causing her to almost spill her coffee when he stopped and said hello.

"I'm glad I ran into you again," the new guy said, laughing, as their first meeting involved crashing grocery carts. "May I join you?" he asked. Annie felt herself blushing as she said that would be great. Introducing himself, Tom McGuire was his name; he told Annie he had just moved to town a few days ago from Chicago. Annie told him her name and that she had come from Maine six years before. Since neither one had any plans for the morning, they sat and chatted through the second cup of coffee, sharing a blueberry muffin.

Before they parted, Tom asked Annie that if she wasn't seeing anyone, would she like to go to dinner tomorrow night, wondering if there was a good restaurant in town. Annie smiled and said that would be lovely, and yes, there was a nice rustic place called the Wary Trout, just down the street. They agreed to meet there at six thirty, with Annie driving herself, just in case the evening did not go well; she was pretty sure that it would. When she got home, she went into her only bathroom and took off all her clothes in front of the full-length mirror, wanting to see if her figure had changed any over the years; at one time in her life, she had been considered very attractive. Up till now, however, she hadn't had a reason to look at herself—as living in this tiny town in northwest Montana, all she ever wore were casual baggy clothes; and not having anyone in her life, what was the point of dressing up? Pleased by what she saw, Annie went into her closet to see if she had something pretty to wear besides her blue jeans, hiking boots, and chamois shirts—items she wore most days. Fortunately, she had brought a few dresses and nice shoes from her home in Maine, so she picked out one with a simple floral design and a pair of flats to match. Next, she dug through what makeup she still had, most of them old and hard but found a nice pink lipstick that would match the print on the dress. But she needed to go to the drugstore for some nail polish, hoping the store also had a nice enticing perfume. She put that on her to-do list for tomorrow.

Annie counted the hours before she would see Tom again, too long she felt, but she kept herself busy neatening up her rustic cabin just in case he wanted to stop by after dinner. Her relationship with her ex-husband, Terry, had been abusive for many years, so it had been a long time since she had, what she hoped, would be a romantic date; she was nervous, to say the least. Remembering back to the day of her first date at sixteen, her mother had told her to not seem too anxious and to be a little late showing up. "Keep them waiting," her mother said with a wink.

CHAPTER 3

Annie woke early; in fact, she hardly slept with the excitement of her first date with Tom. Returning from the drugstore, she sat down and painted her nails; she could not remember the last time she had done that. She checked herself in the mirror many times during the day before it was finally time to head to the restaurant. Taking her mother's advice, Annie showed up at six forty-five, but to her horror, Tom wasn't there. Oh god, she thought, had he gone home or changed his mind, when just then, the door opened; Tom's big frame blocked what light came through behind him. He walked over and gave Annie a polite hug, remarking how lovely she looked and apologizing for being late. She, in turn, telling him she too had just arrived, mentioning that he looked pretty good as well in his turtleneck, pressed khakis, and loafers—a preppy thing for sure.

They took a table in the corner of the tiny restaurant, the only light coming from a small candle between them; it was a cozy spot, to be sure. After ordering, Annie nervously started the conversation by asking Tom how he found this remote little town near Glacier Park. He told her that he had recently retired from being a financial advisor for a boutique firm in Chicago and thought it was time for an adventure. His wife had passed away many years ago, losing a long battle with cancer.

Tom confessed, after a few years, he signed up with a dating service, but it was a disaster, so he threw himself into his work until he decided he had had enough, needing a new place to live out his life. Annie told Tom how sorry she was as his wife, apparently, had been very young when she passed away. Reaching over, she gently squeezed his hand. Tom said he loved the outdoors and had just taken up photography, so he thought this area was perfect for what he hoped would be his last home; Annie wanted that for him, hopefully spending it with her as well. Tom mentioned he has one child, a son in New York, who he loves very much, hoping he would visit soon as going to Chicago from New York, the two cities were too similar. Here, they could do some hikes and explore.

It was Annie's turn to tell her story, being truthful about her past life. She had been a stay-at-home mother, raising two girls; but over the years, her husband had become abusive, somehow convincing the girls that their mother was an adulterer and had belittled their father for years. It wasn't true. Annie told Tom she had not seen her daughters since moving here as they wanted nothing to do with her. Expressing his sorrow, Tom said he hoped she and the girls would get back together someday, soon. That was a wish Annie had had many times since coming out west. She told him about her love of fly-fishing and how peaceful it was just standing in the river while trying to put her past life stresses behind her.

Life is not about waiting for the storms to pass,
but rather it is about how to dance in the rain.

CHAPTER 4

The evening went by way too fast; they closed down the restaurant. It had been a lovely time, the best she could remember. Oddly enough, there were no awkward moments of silence that can happen on a first date as neither stopped talking; each was wanting to learn more about the other. On leaving the restaurant, Tom leaned on his beautiful dark-blue BMW SUV and told Annie that he had had a wonderful time, enjoying her company very much. Annie's knees almost buckled again, but she kept herself upright, telling him how lovely the evening with him had been, thanking him for dinner, and giving him a light kiss on the cheek. Before they parted, Tom expressed an interest in fly-fishing and asked if she would like to teach him; he had never been a fisherman. Annie thought with all the beauty around this area, photography sounded like fun and asked if he would like to teach her how to take that great photo. So with a warm and gentle handshake, it was a deal; they would teach each other what they knew. After some idle chitchat, Tom leaned forward and wrapped his arms around Annie, giving her a wonderful hug. At that moment, her heart felt like it was about to burst; she couldn't wait to see him again. Trading cell numbers and addresses, they bid each other a good night with a light kiss on the lips.

There are many things in life that will catch
your eye, but there are only few things that
will capture your heart—pursue them.

CHAPTER 5

The next day, they met at her friend Brian's fly-fishing shop, taking a lot of time picking out everything he would need to catch that elusive trout. When they were done, Annie said she needed to run a small errand, promising to come over to his house in an hour and then take him to her favorite spot, which just so happens to be behind her little cabin. Annie was happy, giddy to be exact, as not only was Tom handsome, he seemed very kind and gentle. On the way over to his house, she began to make a plan where it would take many sessions in the river teaching him the techniques needed to be successful fishing for trout as Annie wanted to keep seeing this wonderful man; he was a *catch* for sure. As it would turn out, multiple lessons in the river wouldn't be necessary.

After turning on Tom's road, Annie drove through some beautiful aspen and birch trees, coming to an opening where she could see the most gorgeous log cabin she had ever seen. As she was about to knock on the door, it suddenly swung open. There was Tom dressed from head to toe in his new gear.

"How do I look?" Tom asked.

"Like you've done this before," she said, knowing he hadn't. "What a beautiful home. Did you build it?"

Tom mentioned that he found the log cabin online. The builder, someone Annie knew, had run out of money and couldn't finish the interior of the house, so he listed it with Cindy Nagel, the only realtor in town. With some drawings, photos, and a short video, Tom made an offer and overnighted a cashier's check, sealing the deal. When he arrived, he had George, the builder, come by so he could make some revisions, putting in a mudroom and a bread oven in the corner of the kitchen, as well as finishing the interior work needed;

construction would start soon. After a quick tour, Annie followed Tom to his large backyard, where she demonstrated the proper technique of casting, having him try a few before they headed to her place where they would continue the lesson in the river behind her cabin. To say that her house was a bit rustic, compared to Tom's, was an understatement, but that's what she wanted. On the way over to her house, she prayed Tom wasn't a judgmental person, but when he arrived, getting out of his car, he allayed her fears, expressing how much he loved what he saw; he was genuinely sincere.

Walking to the river, Annie gave Tom some basic instructions on entering the water. In that it was March, most of the Flathead River was still frozen in spots, but part of the river meandered over towards her house, creating a small pool that never iced over. The rocks are slippery, so caution is key as the river is cold and you don't want to fall. With baby steps and a staff he had bought at the shop, Tom and Annie made it to a good spot for standing downstream from the rolling water. She told him that trout face upstream so they can get much-needed oxygen while looking for that morsel that would hopefully drop out of the sky. Annie told Tom that they needed to be downstream as trout are wary, and if they see you, they won't take the bait. The casting came next, showing Tom an eleven o'clock to two o'clock movement, letting the line drift down on its own as he lowered the tip. It didn't take long for him to catch on, so Annie showed him how to tie a fly to a leader and cast out the real thing. After a few casts, this man, with the most beautiful blue eyes, caught his first fish; but in his excitement, he pulled up too fast, yanking the hook from the fishes' mouth. Annie then showed Tom how to gently raise the line, allowing the trout to grab the hook. Two casts later, Annie yelled out, "Fish on." Tom gently brought this gorgeous swimmer to his net, whereupon he released the hook, letting his catch swim away; job well done.

CHAPTER 6

They had been on the water for some time, so Annie suggested they head back to the house, her house, as she had bought food for dinner, hoping he would agree to stay; she wanted to impress her new friend with her culinary talents. But as Tom was walking out of the river, he slipped on a rock and fell to his knees, allowing some water to get into his waders. He was okay but wet and cold as he sloshed back to the cabin where Annie handed him a bathrobe to wear while his clothes were drying. When Tom came out of the bathroom, Annie burst into laughter. She had given him a pink robe that was a bit small and short for him, showing off his perfect legs; sexual excitement shot through her body, a wonderful feeling she thought would never happen again.

Sitting by the woodstove, Annie and Tom talked about their day on the river. She was pleased when he asked if they could do that again, soon. With his clothes dry enough to wear and having accepted Annie's dinner invitation, Tom wanted to go change, so he took off with the promise to return in twenty minutes or so. While he was at his house, Annie turned on some Sade love songs and began floating around her kitchen floor as she prepared what she hoped would be a scrumptious dinner for her new friend; she was definitely smitten. It wasn't long before Tom arrived, holding what looked like a very expensive bottle of Merlot and a bouquet of wildflowers that he said he had bought at the grocery store. He was gorgeous in his newly purchased jeans, turtleneck, and polar fleece jacket, purchased yesterday at the Mercantile store in town.

Annie grilled two thick bison steaks, cooked some potatoes and beans from her garden that she had blanched last fall, and for dessert, fresh fruit from the market. Tom was blown away by Annie's cooking, remarking how delicious the steaks were, suggesting she come over to his house sometime so he could show her what he could do in the kitchen; Annie thought she wouldn't care if he burned the meal, she just wanted to keep seeing this amazingly charming man.

It was getting late, so she left the dishes for tomorrow, as not having a dishwasher, Annie didn't want to spend a minute away from who she hoped would be her new special friend. It had only been a couple of days, but Annie thought she was falling in love and hoped he felt something for her as well. Sitting on her big soft couch, they talked well into the night. At one point, Tom slid closer and put his arm around Annie as they watched the lambent flames in her wood-stove. As the evening wore on, they both began to get sleepy after their long day and soon became prone, holding each other warmly; they slept that way all night.

CHAPTER 7

Annie's living room faces east, and as she never wanted curtains, the warm early morning sun's rays streamed through the bay window, gently waking them from a great night's sleep. With their faces only inches apart, they gazed into each other's eyes, at which time they both began to laugh. Tom sat up and tried to apologize, but Annie leaned forward and gave him a sweet kiss on the lips, saying it was okay. She loved it.

After a hearty breakfast of eggs, homemade biscuits, and bacon, Tom needed to head home as he had retained a couple of his clients and wanted to touch base with them; but before he left, he gave Annie a nice hug goodbye. As she watched Tom drive out her road, tears streamed down her face; they were definitely tears of joy. While Tom was taking care of business, Annie made a list of things she needed that she could get locally and things she would have to drive to Kalispell for, a much bigger town that had major box stores and a great hospital system. Taking a chance, she texted Tom to see if he needed anything at Home Depot as she wanted to get more organic soil and compost for her vegetable garden. Tom called a few minutes later and said he would love to go with her, but he needed another hour, maybe, to finish up and would come over as soon as he could. Shortly after they hung up, she was surprised to hear Tom drive up only twenty minutes later, his tires sliding on the gravel as he came to a stop. Before he could knock on the door, Annie came out, throwing her arms around his big frame, giving him a warm embrace, which he accepted willingly. Tom told her one of his clients could wait as he wanted to see her sooner, at which time it was his turn to give her a nice kiss on the lips; his face seemed to be glowing. Love was definitely in the air.

CHAPTER 8

Since Annie had been so kind to show him the tricks of fly-fishing, Tom asked her if there was a camera shop in Kalispell as he needed some new lenses and wanted to set her up with a nice camera so he could teach her a few things that he knows. Fortunately, there was, and it was close to Home Depot. Annie thought how much fun it will be for her to be walking around a store with a gorgeous man by her side after so many years; She and Terry never did that ever, so back home, she shopped alone. Arriving at the big box store, they turned towards the garden shop, and as they were walking, Annie felt Tom's hand take hers, giving her a quick squeeze; this time, her knees did buckle. Tom bought some tools for the outside along with some bushes for the front of the house and ordered a shed to be delivered soon. Annie got her compost and organic soil, and after loading everything they bought, they headed to the camera shop. Tom bought two large lenses and a tripod and then asked the salesman to put together a nice, simple camera and a few lenses for his new, sweet friend. Annie started to say she could pay for it, but Tom put a finger to her lips, hushing her.

On the trip home, Annie leaned over, turning to her new friend, and looked at him lovingly. They talked about anything and nothing for the hour trip back to Hungry Horse, arriving at Tom's house just before dark. As they reached the clearing in front of his log cabin, Tom hit the brakes, causing his SUV to slide on the gravel road. In front of them was a momma bear with her two cubs meandering along towards the woods. Annie could see Tom's eyes almost bulging out of his head, fear showing on his face. Having lived in Montana for several years, Annie had seen her share of bears; and as they were in a safe vehicle, she told Tom to hit his bright lights and drive slowly to the garage, using his automatic door opener to let them inside. After parking his SUV, Tom sat in the car for a few moments as the door closed behind him, waiting for his heart to slow down, at which time he jumped from the car, dashing into the house. Entering the kitchen, all Annie could do was laugh while holding this big scared man, assuring him he was safe.

Tom had never seen a bear of any kind out of captivity, so naturally, he was taken aback. She promised him that she would look and see if there was a lecture, soon, on dealing with bears; and tomorrow, they would go to the local mercantile and get some bear spray to hopefully ward off an attack.

Once Tom got his nerves in check, he started dinner of organic chicken breasts and fresh vegetables he had bought at the farm stand in town. Earlier today, while he was at home working with a client on the phone, he had begun marinating the chicken; they were now ready to grill. Annie was impressed with how he worked in the kitchen and asked if he had always known his way around the pots and pans. The question made Tom's expression change; he became solemn. Annie wondered why she suddenly felt guilty for asking. He told her that his wife, Susie, had been the cook in their family, and he used to watch her create wonderful meals during their thirteen years of marriage. Annie apologized, but Tom walked over and gave her a kiss on the top of her head, stroking her hair, saying it was okay. She couldn't have known.

CHAPTER 9

It had been a long day, another wonderful day, so after a great dinner, Tom took Annie home, dropping off her compost and soil. As he was about to drive away, he said he would like to see her tomorrow, planting a deep kiss on her lips before he drove off. As he did so, Annie laughingly called out to watch out for the bears.

"Not funny," he shot back with a smile, promising to call when he got home.

Tom did call, and they chatted for almost two hours, both lying in their respective beds, both, without saying, wishing they were side by side warmly holding each other again. Annie couldn't believe how her last few days had gone, how happy she was, and was this just a dream? She hoped not, pinching herself just to be sure.

Since she was so excited about her new acquaintance, Annie had to call Claire, her only friend from home, the next morning. She went on and on telling her what a gorgeous man he was—gentle, kind, and loving. Claire was excited but wanted her friend to be cautious, remembering how her ex-husband had been when they first met, turning mean a few years later. She did want her friend to be happy. Annie asked if Claire had seen her girls, and were they okay? Both daughters had completely shut off communication with their mother, not even telling her about their children; that alone brought tears to her eyes when she heard about them through Claire. She said the girls were fine but rejected anything she told them about their mother. In frustration, she stopped trying to convince the girls that their father was the cheater and abuser, not their mother. Annie told Claire she wanted her to come out, and soon, so she could meet this wonderful man and to see her. No date was made, but Claire promised she would fly out when she could.

The past does not always equal the future.

No sooner had Annie hung up with Claire, Tom called and asked if she wanted to take a day to explore. He hadn't been in town very long, so he wanted to see some neighboring areas.

"Of course," Annie said, "that would be great," trying not to sound too excited. Tom arrived soon after, and they took off to Big Fork for a late breakfast and a stroll around that cute little village located at the top of Flathead Lake. After a trip over to Lakeside, they headed to Kalispell, where Tom purchased camping equipment for the two of them at the newly opened REI store; she liked that he wanted to include her in his interests. Annie was excited as she had never camped before, and who better to do that with than Tom, the most amazing man she had ever known.

CHAPTER 10

The next day, Tom and Annie, after a great breakfast at a country diner near the entrance to Glacier Park, drove over to the Avalanche Lake Trail, taking their cameras for a half-day hike. It was a rugged walk, but along the way, Tom pointed out several great photos and showed Annie how the various settings on the camera created different looks. Reaching the lake, they were pleased that because the park had not completely opened for the season, few tourists lined the water's edge, giving them several choice spots to relax and enjoy their new friendship. Annie had packed a nice lunch, so after finding a great log to lean against while they ate, they stared at the beauty of the mountains in front of them. A light breeze sent ripples across the lake, bringing a slight chill to the air, so Tom moved closer, putting his arm around the beautiful woman sitting next to him. With a warm sun beaming down on the two of them, they soon dozed off. When Tom woke, he gently shook Annie awake, saying they needed to head back as it would be dark soon; it could be dangerous. When they finally reached the car, it was dark, but they were safe; it had been another beautiful day.

While driving home, Annie thought Tom seemed more quiet than usual, so she asked if he was okay. He didn't immediately answer her, emitting, instead, a deep sigh. When he did speak, Tom told her how wonderful the last week had been, the best he could remember. He paused before he spoke again, taking a deep breath. *Oh no,* Annie thought, *here comes a* but, *but it didn't come.* When Tom did speak again, he sheepishly asked if she believed in love at first sight, and before she could respond, he asked if she would like to spend the night at his home tonight. Annie was quiet for only a few seconds before she said yes to both questions. She admitted to him that she fell in love the day they had their crash meeting at the grocery store. Apparently, he did too, both laughing at their admissions. Arriving back at Tom's house, they munched on some leftovers from the night before, and as they sat by the fire holding each other lovingly, Annie boldly turned to Tom and said, "It's time for bed."

The two of them nervously stood by Tom's king-size bed, unbuttoning each other's clothes. It had been many years without intimacy for the two of them, but that didn't matter; they knew what to do. Falling on the bed, arms wrapped around each other, they made love many times before sleep took over. When Tom woke in the morning, he saw Annie sitting cross-legged at the end of the bed looking out his big picture window. When she felt the sheets move, she returned to Tom's side; and once again, they made love until dozing off. When Tom finally opened his eyes, he looked over to see Annie gazing at him, a big smile covering her face. They lay in bed a while longer, lightly kissing and telling each other how much in love they thought they were; neither one could believe their recent good fortune. At their age, there's no set time for falling in love.

CHAPTER 11

For the next few weeks, Tom and Annie took many day trips, finding new spots for fishing and photography, plotting what they found on a map they bought at Brian's fly shop. On one of the days, as they were eating lunch at a rustic café along the Flathead River, Tom's cell phone rang. Annie could see her lover's face light up; his son was calling.

"Hey, Boo," Tom's nickname for his son, Ned, "how are ya?"

"Hi, Pop, just thought I'd call to see how you're doing in bear country."

"Everything is great," Tom said. "In fact, beyond wonderful. I love living here, and guess what, I've met the most incredible woman—go figure in such a small town. Her name is Annie, and we've been having a great time exploring the area and getting to know each other." Tom didn't go into every detail of all their explorations! Without hesitation, Ned said, "How wonderful." He was very happy for his dad.

"Can't wait to meet her, text me a photo, when can I come out?"

"You're kidding, of course," Tom said. "You don't need an invitation, anytime."

Annie sat across from her sweet man as he and Ned made plans for a visit this coming weekend, four days away. When they hung up, Annie could see Tom's excitement, so she asked him many questions, wanting to know as much as she could about his son.

When they got home, Annie helped Tom neaten up his house, not that it took long as Tom always kept his home tidy—no dishes allowed in the sink; he was an unusually caring and organized man. For the next three days, Tom seemed even more upbeat with Annie receiving the benefit of his son's pending arrival, getting many more hugs and kisses every day; she, of course, loved the increased attention.

On the day of Ned's arrival, it was a dreary, rainy day as they headed to the airport in Kalispell, but to Tom, you would have thought it was warm and sunny. Bad weather couldn't dampen his spirit as his only child was coming for a visit. Tom told Annie that Ned was a software designer for a large internet company, living and working in New York City. They had seen each other many times since Tom's wife, Ned's mother, had passed away. Having always been close, this will be an extra special time, especially for his dad, who undoubtedly was excited for his son to meet his sweet new friend. Annie was concerned that maybe Ned wouldn't approve of her, taking the place of his mother, but she would soon find out that that wasn't going to be the case.

CHAPTER 12

The plane arrived on time, Tom giving Annie an excited hug. When Ned came through the security door, he ran to his dad, giving him a huge bear hug. They stayed clinched for some time until Ned broke away, turning to Annie and giving her one as well. When they parted, Ned expressed how great it was to meet her, giving her a peck on the cheek. Almost like the time when Annie met Tom, her knees buckled; a big sigh of relief engulfed her. Annie tried to apologize for the weather, but Ned said it didn't matter, he was happy to be here to see his dad and to meet the new friend he had heard so much about. Apparently before coming out, Tom had called his son, telling him a little more about Annie.

As they drove the one-hour drive to Hungry Horse, the weather did clear, and Ned could see the mountain ranges and the beautiful Flathead River; he was definitely impressed. Annie told Ned that the town of Hungry Horse came about when the state built a damn on the Flathead River. Many of the workers stayed after the damn was completed, raising their families in this small town. With only around 1,200 folks in residence, there wasn't much to do. There were only a couple of stores, a gas station, a restaurant and coffee shop, one church, and no movie theater, so meeting someone as wonderful as his dad was not anything Annie had ever expected; lucky for her and him for being near the park with some great fishing grounds, exceptional hikes, and great photography—things they both loved; neither one was complaining, of course.

Pulling up to the house, Ned expressed his approval by what he saw in front of him, anxious to see the inside. After he was settled in his room, he joined Annie and Tom in the living room, warming up to a great fire. Tom had told Ned a lot more about Annie during a lengthy conversation two nights ago when Ned had given his father the flight information, but he turned his attention to this beautiful woman sitting close to his dad, wanting to hear her version as to how they met as he knew his dad had probably embellished his story a bit. Annie told him about the crashing carts and that her heart had skipped a beat the moment she laid eyes on his father. Ned was amazed that in this small rural town, there was a woman as beautiful and seemingly loving as Annie. Tom piped in that he also was shocked, a big smile lighting up his face.

CHAPTER 13

It had been a long day for his son, so Tom suggested they all call it a night and see each other in the morning. Annie thought she should go to her house, but Tom insisted she stay, his son wouldn't mind. The bedrooms were across the house from each other, so Tom and Annie were able to make quiet love before they eventually fell asleep.

As the morning sun peeked through Tom's big window, Annie woke thinking she smelled coffee brewing. Looking over, her man was still asleep, so was she dreaming? Quietly leaving the warm bed, she slipped on her big pink robe and slippers she brought over to Tom's house and headed for the kitchen. As she entered the room, there was Ned getting ready to fry some bacon and toast some bagels he had found in the fridge. Putting down the fork, he walked over and gave Annie a nice hug and kiss on the cheek, saying, "Good morning, pretty lady." Annie was a bit taken aback, but she didn't resist, giving him the same. While they waited for Mr. Wonderful to join them, the two became more acquainted. Finally, Ned told Annie that he had noticed that his dad seemed like his old self, something he had not seen since before his mom died. He admitted that even though his dad and mom had had a good relationship, he thought there was something different in the way he was acting now. Annie piped in that his dad was the most wonderful man she has ever known, and she loved him very much. She told this very handsome young man about her past marriage and that her girls had essentially turned on her, thinking she was a bad person. Ned's dad had brought new life to her being, and she hoped they would live their lives out together. Just then, Tom appeared in the door, still half asleep. Ned served breakfast to the two lovebirds.

CHAPTER 14

After everyone had showered and changed, Annie suggested a quick tour of their little town and then a short drive through part of the park that was open. Ned was, by every indication, impressed not only with where his father had chosen to live but by this lovely lady he had met. Annie showed Tom's son her little cabin and where his dad learned to fly-fish. Ned thought he would like to learn as well, so off they went to Brian's shop to buy more equipment.

Returning to Annie's cabin, Tom, having left his gear at her house, got suited up and headed upstream to a spot Annie had told him about. Leading Ned over the slippery rocks proved to be difficult, but they got to a sandy spot where he could stand without fear of falling into the chilly water. After a quick demonstration, Ned grasped the casting technique well and began the search for his first catch of the elusive trout. Annie, always being a curious person, asked if Ned had a special lady in his life. He said because he worked a sixty-hour week, he hadn't had time to date; but after seeing how happy his dad was, he thought that might be something he would pursue when he got home. Annie thought that he should because he would be some gal's catch of the day being so handsome and charming like his dad. A great shout came from upriver, interrupting their conversation. Tom had caught a nice rainbow; both Annie and Ned gave him a cheer. Turning his attention downstream, Ned stiffened and grabbed Annie's arm. There, about one hundred yards away, was a black bear in the river looking for lunch. Annie laughed and explained that that was a common sight around here, promising to tell Ned later about his father's first encounter with a bear. She explained that because the bear was so far away, if he made his way upriver, they could be in the safety of her cabin before he got too close. Ned mentioned that the last time he saw a bear was when he was about five when his dad took him to the Chicago zoo; he was thrilled by what he was seeing in front of him. On his next cast, his fly landing in a pool just below some rippling water, Ned caught a huge trout, reeling it in with Annie's instructions. Normally, Annie said, she would release the fish, but because this was his first catch, they would have it for dinner tonight. A photo would be taken when they got on dry land; a great picture for Tom's wall in the kitchen.

CHAPTER 15

The night was spent in more conversation over a great dinner of the rainbow trout, potatoes, and veggies from Annie's garden when Ned blurted out that he really misses his dad, and seeing how beautiful it was in Montana, he wanted to move out to be near them both. In his business, he can write programs from anywhere if there was a good internet connection. Oddly enough, for this remote area, there was a very strong signal, so Ned started making plans to have his equipment sent out as soon as possible. Tom was, of course, excited by that prospect, so too was Annie. Ned also thought he would like to come back for Thanksgiving, which brought another cheer from his dad. As that day was several months away, Ned promised his dad he would begin to make arrangements with his company in New York to make the move out west, possibly after Christmas. Annie was so excited for Tom but sad that she didn't think her daughters would ever come out even for a visit.

CHAPTER 16

The day before Tom's son was to leave and go back to the big city, Annie, once again, found herself alone with Ned in the kitchen. After he poured them both a cup of coffee, he asked about her daughters and could he do anything to help reunite them. Ned then said something she never expected, which made her heart swell.

"Annie, you need to know my dad means everything to me. My mom died when I was almost fourteen, leaving dad to take care of me alone. I started to fall into depression, so he did some research and found an outdoor school dealing with many of life's issues. He took me to Bethel, Maine, putting me into a two-week course with a group called Outward Bound."

Annie interjected, saying that she knew that town as she had lived only a few hours away.

"When Dad had to leave me, I was crying and scared, not wanting him to go. I was afraid I might get lost and never see him again. When the course was over, my father was there waiting for me, having driven all the way back from Chicago. To say I was a different kid after my trip, was an understatement, a magical transformation to say the least. I was totally a more confident and self-assured boy. Arriving home, after many hours of great conversations on the drive back, we both thought that a year away at a boarding school would be helpful to further build my independence and confidence, so I went to this amazing school called Avon Old Farms in Connecticut. During that year, there wasn't a family function that he didn't come to. He would even just show up for no reason, so I saw him a lot. I had a great year academically and athletically and loved that school so much, I went there for the next three years, graduating with honors and receiving a scholarship to play lacrosse at Penn State. After a year and a half there, I called my dad and asked if he could come to campus as I needed his advice. He flew in the next day, and we talked for some time about why I needed to see him. I told him I thought I would be more successful learning by doing and that I wanted to drop out of school. Dad knew that I had always been a sensible kid, so he agreed, asking me what I wanted to do. I had always been interested in computers and the programs that bring the world to almost every home, so we researched companies that had a great training program. Because Dad was in the financial world, he had his researchers at the brokerage firm where he worked send him information on all public and private companies that made these programs. I decided on a firm in New York that had worldwide connections.

"Annie," Ned continued, "who I am as a person and all my successes so far in my life are because of what my dad did for me. He sacrificed so much. I love him more than anyone in the world."

Annie was blown away by what Ned had just confided with her. If it was possible to be more in love with this wonderful man, she was at that moment.

"Oh, Ned, I'm not surprised as your father is the most caring, loving man I have ever known. I know it has been only a short time that we have been together, but I have never loved a man like I love your dad. He's special."

Continuing, Ned said, "Annie, I've only known you for a few days, but I can see that you are a wonderful person, and you've made my dad so happy. I love you for that as I know he has been lonely for so long! There's no doubt that he cares deeply for you, and I believe, if all goes well, that you two will probably get married someday. Having said that, would it be okay if I didn't call you Annie, but called you Mom now, rather than later?"

Ned had felt so sorry that this beautiful lady didn't have her two girls in her life, and besides, he thought it would be great to have someone he could call Mom again, after fifteen years.

Annie was so taken by what Ned said, her eyes welled up with tears as she leaned over and gave him a big kiss.

"I'd like that very much," she replied. "I do hope your father and I will spend the rest of our lives together as, for me, he is an angel sent by God."

They sat for some time chatting before his sleepy-eyed dad stuck his head in the kitchen, wondering what the two of them were talking or scheming about. Annie was the first to speak, telling Tom what his son had asked of her and what his prediction of their future was going to be. All Tom could do was give his son the wary eye, smiling, while he poured himself a cup of coffee.

The rest of the day was spent in Whitefish, where Tom bought his son some necessary clothing for the colder weather when he returns for Thanksgiving. Looking around town, Ned thought Whitefish looked like a fun place to live and work, plus being five times bigger than Hungry Horse, he would, no doubt, meet more people his age. Since the town is at the base of Big Mountain Ski slope, one of the best in the country, Ned figured he could slip away for a half day from work and enjoy the slopes whenever he wanted. He had learned to ski with friends while in boarding school, so he was happy to see there was a place nearby to glide down a mountain. Before leaving town, Tom, Annie, and Ned popped into a real estate office to register with an agent, letting her know that they would call when they are ready to look at some homes.

CHAPTER 17

The next day, Tom and Annie sadly took "their" son to the airport. Lots of hugs and promises between them before Ned went through the security gates. On the way home, Annie could see Tom was a bit sad, so she reassured him his son would return in a few months, and eventually for good. She also told him what a great parenting job he had done raising Ned as he is just a wonderful young man, one of the best she has ever known. In the back of her mind, she thought her goddaughter Betsy, Claire's daughter, would love to meet Ned someday; she would plant the seed soon after talking with Claire.

Rather than cooking at home when they got back to town, they went to the Wary Trout, the place of their first official date. Tom and Annie talked about the last couple of days and Ned's idea to come live nearby, which, of course, made Tom very happy. They also spoke about her girls but didn't come up with a solution to getting them together. Arriving home, Tom's home, it was still early, but they went to bed anyway, enjoying each other's bodies for some time until sleep took over; no doubt they were deeply in love as intimacy was still so very exciting.

The following morning, Annie went to the little, but well-stocked, grocery store and happened to see a poster about a lecture in the park on how to counter a bear attack. Since she had never fully learned what to do herself, Annie thought they should both go this Saturday to find out how to keep those big animals away and stay safe.

The lecture was very informative and helpful, but before they left, Tom went up to the ranger who had given the talk and told him about his love of the outdoors. Ranger Brad was impressed with Tom's knowledge of hiking and nature and thought he should apply for a part-time ranger job that was available. Before they left the park, they stopped at the ranger station where Tom filled out an application. Two days later, Tom got a call from Brad offering him the job, which he accepted, willingly.

CHAPTER 18

Since Annie had already brought most of her clothes over to Tom's house and had taken over a small area in the master closet, she changed into some casual clothes and went to cook dinner while Tom built another great fire in his beautiful Montana stone fireplace. With dinner ready, Annie started to walk into the living room when she suddenly stopped in her tracks. In front of her were pink rose petals strewn on the floor leading to the coffee table that had a vase holding twelve beautiful Queen Anne's roses. Tom turned to her as she walked over to the couch and got on one knee. He was holding a small velvet box and, upon opening it, asked if she would honor him by being his bride. He explained that even though it had only been a short time since they met, he felt he couldn't live without her and hoped she would say yes to his proposal. All Annie could do was put her hands over her mouth as she nodded her head up and down, tears streaming down her cheeks. After Tom slipped a beautiful diamond and Montana sapphire ring on her finger, they embraced each other for a long time. It so happened that when the three of them were in Whitefish, Tom had excused himself while they were with the realtor, leaving for a short time to go a beautiful jewelry store called McGough, and bought the ring; Annie had no idea. Later, lying in bed, the only wearable thing to be found on either one was that gorgeous ring on Annie's finger. They held each other passionately, exploring every inch of their bodies before sleep, once again, took over.

In the morning, Tom's eyes peeked out from the comforter at another great-looking day. It could have been snowing heavily or raining cats and dogs, it just didn't matter because at this moment, he was in love, something he didn't think would ever happen again.

ride back to Hungry Horse was amusing as the young one was rolling around the back of Tom's car or trying to get in the front seat with Annie. They both laughed the whole way home.

Before they got back to Hungry Horse, they took a detour over to Whitefish, to a dog store that handled only the best foods on the market. While there, they bought puppy chow for the lab and a bag of the healthiest food for the older dog. Bowls, leashes, and dog beds were the next purchases along with a crate for training the little one when he gets to his new home; needless to say, with all the purchases, the golden ended up front with Annie for the short ride home. Arriving back at the house and letting the newest member of the family out of the car, all he could do was run around the yard, stopping occasionally to scratch his back on the lawn. After corralling this incredibly fast dog, they got him inside, putting down in the corner of the kitchen the ergonomic bed they bought, and then fed him. They guessed he was excited because he didn't just eat his meal, he devoured it in seconds. Annie and Tom hadn't yet given this puppy—all dogs are puppies—a name yet. In China, he was called Kester, but the foster parents said because he had been caged for almost all his life, he probably didn't know his name, so Annie decided to give him one that was close, *Cooper*.

If one has never loved a dog, then part
of their soul remains unawakened.

CHAPTER 20

Three weeks passed by quickly, so off they went to get the little one; Cooper was excited for another car ride. Arriving at the kennel, he played with all the puppies as Tom signed the papers and paid for their new "child." They decided on the name Barley for this adorable yellow boy. To say the least, the ride home was a riot with both boys rolling around in the back of the car.

It was decided that whenever either Annie or Tom were working, the other one would take the boys out for some training or just to enjoy the great weather before winter sets in. Cooper seemed to love his little brother, wrestling on the floor or chasing a ball with him in the backyard. When they were all together, the new parents would take the puppies for a long walk; Barley was carried most of the time as his little legs couldn't keep up. They would also take the pups to town to socialize with other dogs who were on a stroll with their owners. What Tom and Annie hadn't figured on was that their lazy days lying in bed early in the morning were over for a while as both dogs would make a fuss in the morning with Cooper dashing in from his comfy bed in the kitchen and Barley yelping to get out of his crate as they either needed to go out or be fed—mostly to be fed. Annie remarked it reminded her when her girls were very young and did the same thing; Tom dittoed that as Ned was a handful. No worries as they were enjoying these beautiful dogs and embraced all the commotion during the day. It felt good to be parents again even though their kids had four legs. Annie thought the puppies had, if possible, brought her and Tom even closer together.

CHAPTER 21

Weeks went by, October had arrived. Tom was enjoying giving flora and fauna classes to the many tourists in the park. Annie had thought that since her man was working part-time that she should find something to do while he was in the park; the puppies would be okay for a few hours, so she stopped by Brian's shop to see if he needed any help. It just so happens he had bought a float boat, and he was getting calls for guide trips down the Flathead and could use her while he was on the water; she can start in two days.

When Tom got home that day, he was excited about Annie's new job, figuring that they could get a discount on fishing equipment, not that money was an issue with Tom—he had plenty. Another week went by, and Tom's job was winding down as the park would close soon. He told Annie he wanted to do one last hike before the snows come. As she was working at the shop, she couldn't go with him but asked if one of his ranger friends would be going along. Tom said no, that it was only a short hike and that he would be home way before dinner. Having lived here long enough to know the perils of solo hiking, especially this time of year, Annie begged him to wait until she could go along, but Tom insisted, he would be fine. The next day, Tom stuffed his hiking gear into his big pack, threw in some food and water in case he got hungry, and took off, giving Annie a warm hug and a kiss; she, once again, begged him not to go alone. Tom went anyway, which made Annie mad at him for the first time ever. Not liking the way she felt, she told herself he would be fine; Tom was a sensible man.

CHAPTER 22

All day, while at work, Annie had a bad feeling and couldn't wait to go home and find her man at the house, safe and sound. She had tried to reach Tom by cell phone many times during the day, but the cell service connection in the park was spotty, so she left multiple messages asking him to call her ASAP. Annie finally closed the shop and drove home, praying that Tom's car would be in the garage; but as she approached the house, she could see it was dark. Panic began to set in. She called again, but Tom still didn't pick up. He had told her he would probably drive up to the Grinnell Trail and walk that route for a few hours, but because of the time of year, the rangers close the gate at Avalanche Lake at dark. Avalanche was the trail where they had hiked a few weeks back. Tom did have a key in case he got back too late, so he could let himself out, but Annie didn't, and the hike to Grinnell Trail was over two miles from the gate. It was also dark and too dangerous as bears were aggressively looking for food before hibernating, and they are predominantly nocturnal; she felt helpless as to what to do.

It was almost 9:00 p.m., and still no call. Annie was crying now, feeling something horrible had happened to her lover, so she called Brad, the head ranger and one of Tom's buddies, and told him her fears. Brad said that there wasn't anything he could do at this late hour, but he assured her he would head up to the trail at first light. Annie said she wanted to go with him and would meet him at the park entrance. Sleep was impossible; she couldn't even cry, so she paced all night.

Before the sun came up, Annie took off in her Jeep to meet Brad at the gate. Shortly after arriving, he showed up, and they took off in his park-issued vehicle and headed to the Grinnell Trail parking lot. As they rounded the sharp curve on the Going to the Sun Road, they could see the parking lot was empty; Annie immediately burst into tears. Where could he be? If he had driven down the road, they would have seen him; they hadn't. Brad got on his two-way radio and called the office requesting that a search party be formed, adding a helicopter as well. Since the park is huge, Tom could be anywhere, but "Where?" was the question.

The search went on all day, covering several trail areas near the Grinnell; but by 4:00 p.m., with sunlight dwindling, Brad called off the search, much to the dismay from Annie. He explained to her that most of the trails in the park are hard enough to maneuver in daylight, so it was not safe to continue in the dark.

Annie drove home having a great deal of trouble seeing the road through the tears that filled her eyes and streamed down her face; she again arrived at an almost empty house. The puppies greeted her lovingly, so she let them out and then fed them before heading to the couch after building a small fire; the boys were lying next to her. It was again a long night as she lay there thinking of a million scenarios as to where he could be. The only comforting thing was she put her head on the throw pillow that was on Tom's side of the couch; she could smell him.

Brad called the next day asking if she wanted to come search again, but she declined, opting instead to cuddle with her puppies, hoping he would call with good news or Tom would show up. Another day passed, and by this time, Annie was convinced Tom wasn't coming back. She had cried so much over the last couple of days, she had no more tears. Brad came by and sat with her, saying they weren't giving up but that she needed to prepare for the worst. With the night temps dropping into the thirties and lower, Tom may be the victim of hypothermia, or he had fallen to his death somewhere in the park; they just didn't know where. The other, more grizzly thought was that he had met a bear on the trail. None of these thoughts made Annie feel better, but she knew she had to accept them as possible reasons her man had not returned.

CHAPTER 23

October 11, 2018

It had now been three days since she last held Tom; hope had all but disappeared. Annie finally called Claire telling her what she thinks had happened and that she didn't feel she could go on. Alarmed, her best and only friend from back home tried to calm her down, promising she would be on the next flight out. Annie hung up and called Ned, telling him the same, but she had to leave a voice message giving him the bad news, also giving him Claire's telephone number; she wasn't sure why. Knowing what she thought she had to do, Annie got the puppies settled, but before she left the house, she called Brian, asking him to stop by and look after the dogs, leaving him feeding instructions. She told him she had to go to Kalispell and would be gone all day; but that, of course, was a lie—she wouldn't be back. Annie left a note to Claire and Ned apologizing for what she had done, left her cell phone and purse on the table, and went to the park.

Annie drove up to Grinnell Trail, the place where Tom said he would be hiking. Not sure exactly what she was going to do, she walked until she found a place to stand, deciding then to leap to her death, ending her pain. The wind began to howl, making hearing and standing difficult. She didn't even hear the helicopter flying overhead.

"What am I waiting for?" Annie asked herself as she inched forward towards the edge. One more foot, and it was over. As she was about to take her last step, someone grabbed her from behind, pulling her away from certain death.

"What are you doing! Let me go. I want to die," she screamed. Turning around, she saw Brad holding her.

"Annie," Brad yelled above the wind, "Tom's alive. We found him over on the Avalanche trail. He's in bad shape, but the EMTs said he will be okay in time. He has a broken right leg and some lacerations on his face, a broken left arm, some badly bruised ribs, and he possibly suffered a concussion. He's on the way to the hospital in Kalispell by helicopter."

Annie threw her arms around Brad's neck and wept violently. She could hardly believe what she had just heard.

"Take me to him, Brad, I have to see him."

Brad told her he had a state trooper waiting for her at the park entrance who would, with sirens blaring, get her to the hospital as fast as he could.

On the way down, with one of Brad's rangers following in Annie's Jeep, she asked him a million questions. Why did he change his location, how did he survive three days in the cold, was he suffering when they found him, was he alert? Brad did his best to answer all her catechizing.

"Annie, before they put him on the copter, Tom told me to tell you he loves you and was sorry, he'll see you later."

When they got to where the state police car was waiting, Annie gave Brad a hug and a kiss and made him promise to never tell Tom or anyone what she had been about to do on the cliff; he assured her it was their secret.

CHAPTER 24

The nice trooper followed Annie to her home as she wanted to leave her car, check on the dogs, and grab her cell phone to call Claire; in her haste, she forgot her purse. As suspected, Claire had called, sounding frantic as to where her friend was, telling her she was on her way, arriving later tonight. Ned also called, saying he would be coming as soon as he can get a flight. On the way to the hospital, Annie called Brian, asking him to continue looking after the dogs; she would be home even later than she thought. She also called Claire and Ned, telling them the good news, leaving messages for both of them. The trooper, whose name was Rick, did his best to keep Annie from thinking about Tom as he drove as fast as he could along the country roads between the mountains heading to Kalispell and the regional hospital. On the way, he got a call from central giving him an update on Tom's condition; he was at the hospital and being taken into surgery.

Thirty minutes later, they arrived at the hospital. Annie thanked the trooper and made a beeline to the front desk asking where she could find her husband; as they weren't married yet, it was only a little white lie. When she got to the third floor by elevator, the head nurse took her to an ICU room where she could wait; Tom was still in surgery.

It was some time before the door opened, and two orderlies brought Tom in on a stretcher, still unconscious from the propofol, but he should wake soon. Since Annie hadn't slept in days, she put her head on Tom's bed and immediately dozed off. She didn't know how long she had been asleep, but she felt something stroking her head. As she looked up, she saw Tom lying on his back, his left arm and lower right leg in casts; his right arm was stroking her hair. His smile made Annie break into an uncontrollable sob. With tears raining down, Annie stood up and gingerly wrapped her arms around her sweet, battered man, kissing his lips and face where his skin wasn't scarred from his fall. Still groggy, Tom tried to speak, but Annie put her fingertips on his lips, shushing him. She said she loved him so much but that she was really mad at him right now; a serious discussion, she promised, would come later once he was home. All Tom could do was blink and move his head slowly up and down. He was able to mouth the word *dogs*, and Annie assured him they were being taken care of by Brian. He also asked if she had called Ned; she had, of course.

They held each other for some time until a nurse came in to take Tom's vitals and fill Annie in on what was done in the operating room. The nurse assured her that he would, in time, recover completely, but he would have limited mobility for several weeks. To Annie, that was okay; Tom was alive, and that's all that mattered.

Tom's doctor came in to see how his patient was doing. Annie felt compelled to give him a hug, thanking him for taking care of her man. While the doctor was checking on Tom, she called Claire, leaving a message to call her when she landed; a short time later, her friend did call. Annie told Claire to take a cab to the hospital and to call her when she got there, asking her to hold the cab. Annie called Ned, leaving a message, telling him she was with his dad and that he was badly hurt but alert. It was close to the time when visiting hours were over, so when Claire called, she was downstairs. Annie gave Tom many kisses and told him she would be back tomorrow, telling her battered love, with a wink, not to leave the hospital for any reason.

Annie ran to Claire after getting off the elevator, hugging her friend as hard as she could. It had been six years since they last saw each other, thanking her for coming; then she saw Betsy, her goddaughter, Claire's daughter, standing nearby, a big smile on her face—what a great surprise. The three girls hugged again before getting in the cab to go back to the airport where Claire had to use her credit card to rent a car since, when Annie stopped at the house before coming to the hospital, she absently left her purse on the kitchen counter. On the way home, with Betsy driving as Annie could barely keep her eyes open, she thanked them both for coming; it meant the world to her. During the drive, Annie filled Claire and Betsy in on what had happened, leaving out the part of her failed attempt at suicide; the only person that would ever know was Brad, and he was sworn to secrecy.

CHAPTER 25

Arriving at Tom's house, both girls were exhausted after their long day of flying, so after getting the excited puppies in their beds, and after some small talk and more hugs, all three turned in for the night. The old Maine adage, you can't get there from here, is true as getting to Kalispell usually takes three planes and at least thirteen hours with the time change.

Annie slept longer than she wanted, wondering when she woke, why the dogs hadn't been fussing. Entering the kitchen, she saw Claire had made coffee, and Betsy was on the floor playing with the puppies. They had let both boys out and fed them, following the instructions she had left for Brian; Annie guessed they liked "Aunt Betsy." During breakfast, the girls made a plan on going to the hospital after taking the rental car back to the airport. Betsy said she would stay with the pups, seeing them later when they returned with Tom's son, who was arriving later that evening. Annie was told when she left the hospital the night before that she wouldn't be able to see Tom until late morning and maybe not until around 1:00 p.m., so Annie showed Claire and Betsy around Tom's house and then took them over to her little cabin; both girls loved what they saw. After an early lunch, Claire followed Annie, in Tom's SUV, to the airport, dropping off the rental car, then the girls drove over to the hospital to see Tom. On the way, Annie asked why Betsy came, thinking, after what she told Claire about Ned, that maybe the two should meet someday; all Claire did was smile and say, "Betsy loves her godmother and wants to be there for her." As for meeting Ned, she just winked and smiled. When Annie got to Tom's room, she thought she should go in first just to make sure it was okay for him to meet her only real friend. This certainly wasn't the way she wanted Tom to meet her

49

best buddy, but it would be okay; they'd have something to laugh about in the years to come.

Entering the room, Annie saw that Tom was sitting up, smiling, immediately stretching his arms out as best he could, hoping to get a hug. Annie obliged, being careful not to squeeze too hard as his ribs were wrapped and his left arm was covered in plaster; his broken right leg was elevated by a pulley system. All Annie could do was laugh and cry at the same time. Yesterday she had all but given up hope of seeing Tom alive, and now she was holding the most special man she had ever known, kissing him lightly on the lips. Tom told her that the doctor had just been in and said he was doing well under the circumstances and could probably go home in a couple of days; Tom's lobbying for a tomorrow release apparently had failed.

Annie told Tom, "Ned's coming today, but he will arrive too late for a visit. You'll see your son tomorrow. And oh, by the way, my best friend, Claire, is outside in the hallway." Tom, with Annie's help, carefully sat up, pretending to spruce himself and said to bring her in. As Claire came into the room, he did his best crippled look, causing Claire to laugh and Annie to lightly smack his good arm in exasperation. Getting a nice peck on the cheek from Claire, Tom said how grateful he was that she came to be with her friend.

They spoke for some time when Annie's phone rang; it was Ned. She handed the phone to Tom, and the two men cried and laughed before saying goodbye, both anxious to see each other tomorrow. Ned was in O'Hare Airport in Chicago and would arrive around eight at Glacier Park International Airport.

At six o'clock, after a long conversation about what Tom had been through, Annie and Claire said their goodbyes and headed off to find a place for dinner; hospital food didn't excite them much.

CHAPTER 26

Ned's plane arrived early. Annie was excited to see her "son" walk through the security gate, running over to give him a hug and kiss, holding him tight for some time. Breaking their connection, he turned to Claire and did the same, thanking her for calling; he was happy to meet her. On the way home, about an hour drive, Annie told Ned as much as she could remember about the last few days and that she was excited for him to meet Claire's daughter, who was home watching over the four-legged "children" who Ned had not yet met.

Betsy saw the car lights peering through the trees, so she opened the front door, letting the puppies out, and stood on the front step, ready to greet Ned, this wonderful guy her mom and Annie had told her about. Once inside, Betsy and Ned met more formally, Ned doing his usual, giving her a hug; what a chip off the old block, as they say. He was hungry from a long flight, so they all headed to the kitchen, Claire and Annie pulling out some leftovers while Betsy and Ned played with the puppies, who were happy to meet the new guy. It had been a long day, so after dinner, the gang all retired to their bedrooms, Claire and Betsy sharing one of the guest rooms for the night, Ned taking the other.

Everyone woke early, the pups the first to rise, raising a ruckus, waking every human in the house. When Annie came into the kitchen, she saw Claire but no dogs, Betsy, or Ned.

"Where are the kids?" Annie asked.

"Taking a walk down the driveway with the dogs," Claire replied, winking at Annie. "They seem to be hitting it off."

"Boy, would that be great, girlfriend. He's as handsome and loving as his father—you know, that beat-up guy in the hospital?" She was laughing at herself. "How cool would that be if they became a couple." Only time will tell, she thought.

Like Ned, Betsy didn't have anyone special in her life as prospects in her little seaside town in Maine were few, and the ones that were available just didn't make her checklist. Arriving back at the house, with the dogs' tails wagging and their tongues slobbering, Betsy and Ned got coffee and sat at the breakfast table staring intently at each other while making small talk. Later in the morning, Claire and Betsy decided to stay at the house while Annie and Ned drove up to the hospital to see his dad.

CHAPTER 27

On the ride, Annie spoke first.

"So, Ned, it looks like you and Betsy are hitting it off."

"She's a neat gal, Mom," Ned said. "Betsy is very inquisitive and has a great sense of humor, not to mention she's gorgeous, just like her mother. I like her. I hope to see her when we go back to the east coast. I'm sure it's an easy flight to Portland from JFK or vice versa. She said she hasn't been to New York since she was little, so a trip down would be fun."

"I had told Claire all about you and how I thought you were handsome and, just like your father, charming and kind," Annie confided.

"Thanks, Mom, I haven't addressed the idea of my moving out here with her as it might be some time before that happens. I don't want to put a damper on our new friendship since we just met."

Walking into Tom's room, all Ned could do was look at his father all plastered up and shake his head. Before he gave his dad an awkward hug, he spoke sternly to him.

"Do you know the anxiety you caused us both? What were you thinking, hiking by yourself?" Ned was sounding like he was the dad scolding his young son.

Tom didn't say anything, only reaching out wanting to apologize, but couldn't find the words while getting choked up seeing his son standing there. Ned walked over, bent down, and gave his father a kiss, telling him he loved him and was happy to see him alive.

"I'm sure Mom has told you already, you are never to go on a hike, either short or long, alone again, do you understand?"

Tom was finally able to talk. "She has, and not that it means anything now, but when I bought all my gear, I purchased a heat-sealing blanket that you wrap around yourself, holding your body heat in. I also had plenty of protein and tablets you put in the water to prevent giardia in case my water supply got low. Fortunately, there was a small stream I could reach to get water. I had everything I needed to have a good hike. What I didn't factor in was falling into a ravine and getting my leg wedged. I promise I will never do that again."

Annie told Tom about the possible budding friendship between his son and Betsy, getting Tom's immediate approval. From what he'd heard, Betsy is quite the looker and very sweet. The nurse came in and took Tom's vitals, followed by the surgeon. He was glad Annie was there so he could give her care instructions once Tom is home. "He will be in a wheelchair and on crutches, but only for short periods for at least several weeks," he said. "Both his right leg and his left arm need to be wrapped in plastic bags while bathing, keeping the plaster dry, but what's most important is for Tom's leg to be elevated when sitting or lying down—something he has to do most of the day and night." Annie's first thought was she wouldn't be able to cuddle with her man for several weeks, but she was immediately ashamed of her selfish thought; Tom was alive, and that was more important. With a wink, the surgeon also told Tom he couldn't hike for at least three months and only on flat ground—short hikes only. Before he left, Tom asked when he could go home. The word was if he continued to improve the rest of the day, he could possibly be released tomorrow—great news.

CHAPTER 28

Tom seemed weary, so Annie and Ned kissed him goodbye with a promise to come back tomorrow, hopefully for the last time. Arriving home, Annie and Claire took off to the grocery store to get dinner, not getting an argument from the young kids. She told Claire about her conversation with Ned; Claire, of course, was pleased. She said Betsy thought Ned was the nicest man she had ever met, so who knows where this was going? Just for fun, the girls took some extra time at the store deciding on what to put on the table so their kids could be alone a bit longer.

Remembering what the surgeon had said about Tom's need to keep his leg elevated, Ned and Annie, with help from Betsy and Claire, carried Tom's super-equipped La-Z-Boy chair into the bedroom, lining it up as close as they could get to the left side of the bed so Annie could hold her man's right hand during the night.

After building a nice fire, another trait Ned inherited from his father, they all sat around talking about the last couple of days and how lucky Tom was. Annie started to cry thinking back to what she almost did, feeling ashamed again. When Claire asked if she was okay, all Annie could do was say that the last week, for her, was the worst week she had experienced in many years; she was glad it turned out okay—well, sort of. It was early, not even 8:00 p.m., but Annie was needing some alone time, so she excused herself, taking Cooper with her to bed.

Claire, Betsy, and Ned sat up for some time. The main conversation was, of course, about Annie. How could they help her, what one thing could they do to make her happy again? Ned came up with the best thought, which was figure out how to convince Annie's daughters that they have been wrong about their mother all these years.

55

Claire piped in that she had tried many times, but her girls didn't want to listen to anything she had to say about their father. Ned also mentioned that it would be great if Claire and Betsy could come out for Christmas; they thought that was a wonderful idea. Certainly, by then, Tom would be back in better health, and they could all have a great time. Betsy and Ned could go skiing, and the big kids could do what big kids do, whatever that is. Claire said she would make airline reservations in the morning. Since she and Betsy have plans for Thanksgiving, they would return a week before Christmas. Ned explained that because he had made the unexpected trip out for his dad, he would not come back for Thanksgiving.

The next morning, Annie came into the kitchen having had a good night's sleep, finding everyone sitting at the table drinking coffee waiting for her to arrive. They told Annie what they had discussed after she went to bed the night before, and she was thrilled, hugging both Claire and Betsy; and since it was Ned's idea about them all coming out for Christmas, he got a huge hug and a kiss for making her so happy. To have her best friend, goddaughter, Ned, and Tom together for such a special holiday was the best medicine ever. Soon after breakfast, Annie and Ned left for the hospital; Claire and Betsy would use Annie's Jeep to go to Whitefish to shop. They would all see each other later.

CHAPTER 29

Arriving at the hospital, Annie and Ned were instructed to go to the surgeon's office before visiting Tom. When seated, they got the news they were hoping for: Tom can home today but not before the doctor went over his previous instructions again, handing Annie a sheet of paper with everything she needed to know and more. He also gave her prescriptions for medicines Tom will need to be comfortable while he heals as well as where to get a wheelchair and crutches.

Entering Tom's room, they found him sitting up dressed in a hospital-issued gown with a blanket he could take with him. The clothes he had when he went for his hike had been thrown out; they had been cut up as the EMTs needed to address his wounds before they airlifted him to the hospital. What items that were still wearable were in a plastic bag in his lap. With a smile from ear to ear, Tom said, "Let's roll."

Ned drove while Tom lay flat in the front seat that was pushed all the way back; Annie sat behind him, stroking his head, giving him a few kisses. After a quick stop at the medical supply store near the hospital to get his new wheelchair and crutches, they headed to Columbia Falls to fill the prescriptions for Tom, and then they drove home. Annie called Claire telling her they were all on their way, tears of joy streaming down her face.

The girls were outside with the dogs when Tom's SUV came to a stop in front of the house. Like trying to open a sardine can, Ned and Annie gingerly extracted Tom from the front seat, helping him into his new mode of transportation for the next few weeks. The puppies were happy to see their poppa, clamoring for attention; little Barley was getting on his dad's lap as they rolled him into the house, smothering him with kisses.

There is no better doctor in the world
than a puppy licking your face.

Once inside, Annie introduced Tom to Betsy; a few hugs followed. No one was cooking dinner tonight, so Annie called in an order from the Trout, which was eaten casually in the living room by the fire. Ned told his dad about the Christmas plans and that he would skip coming out for Thanksgiving; Tom was thrilled.

The next day, Annie called George, the builder, explaining what had happened and Tom's handicap condition, asking him if he could come over and build a low ramp so she could get Tom's wheelchair over the threshold at the back door. Apparently, the whole town had heard about Tom's accident, as had the folks who work in the park because the mailman arrived leaving off a big box filled with cards and letters and offers of food. Annie thought the cards should keep Tom busy for a while.

In that Tom needed to rest, the next few days found Betsy and Ned taking side trips, spending hours away from the house, leaving Annie and Claire home with the puppies and the "invalid." Claire had bought some board games in Whitefish the day before at a toy store, so the two of them played with Tom, who did take a few naps in between games.

CHAPTER 30

A week had passed; it was time for the girls from Maine to fly home, so with best wishes and hugs all around and the promise to come back for Christmas, Ned drove Claire and Betsy to the airport while Annie stayed home with Tom and the puppies.

At the airport, Betsy and Ned stood away from Claire, hugging and talking while she got their boarding passes; there were even a few tears from both. Ned would stay a few more days and then head back to New York, promising he would see Betsy soon. As they walked to the security area, Claire had a great idea; since Ned had made an unscheduled flight out and was not coming back before Christmas, he should come up to Maine for Thanksgiving. Ned had no plans, so he accepted the invitation; Betsy, of course, was thrilled. It was Ned's turn for a great idea. He suggested that Claire and Betsy should fly down to New York and they all fly to Montana together for Christmas; he would meet them at Kennedy Airport. With a hug from Claire and an extra hug and kiss from Betsy, the girls turned and walked to their plane, Betsy turning several times to blow Ned a kiss goodbye; no doubt, they were both smitten.

When he arrived back at the house, Ned immediately wanted to know how his dad was doing. Tom was watching Annie cooking dinner when he walked in. Ned laughed as he saw his dad trying to do wheelies in his chair, leg outstretched, smiling as he maneuvered around the very large room; he was driving Annie crazy.

"Someone is in a good mood," Ned remarked. "I guess he never did grow up."

His expression then turned serious. "You need to cool it, Dad, you have a lot of healing to do. Who do you think you are, Mario Andretti? You have the most amazing woman now and a son who thinks you walk on water, so for you to take off on a selfish solo hike in the park that has dangerous terrain, was unconscionable. Never ever do that again. Is that understood?"

With that, Ned took the puppies outside for a walk—as it turned out, a long walk. Tom was stunned, he had never seen his son so mad, not even after his mom died. Looking at her man, Annie saw tears rolling down his face; he had begun to sob uncontrollably. It was some time before he said a word, looking at his beautiful lady. When he spoke, he said he was so very sorry, and could she ever forgive him. The only thing he could think to do was wheel himself into the bedroom.

CHAPTER 31

It was twenty minutes before Ned walked through the back door with the dogs. Annie was curled up on the couch wrapped in a heavy fleece blanket; she too had been crying. Ned rebuilt the fire while he waited for water to boil, finally bringing in two cups of tea for Annie and himself; Annie sat up and moved over, hugging her wonderful new "son."

"I'm sorry, Mom, I shouldn't have yelled at Dad, but I'm sure, like me, he scared the hell out of you, and that really pissed me off. You are the most wonderful person. You deserved more respect."

"Oh, honey, your dad didn't mean to upset us, he just didn't think anything would happen. Did you mean what you said before about his love for me is stronger than what he had with your mom? I hope that doesn't upset you. I know you must have loved her deeply."

"Of course I loved her, but Mom was sick for so long before she died. Her energy level was that of an eighty-year-old, doing her best under the circumstances. It certainly had a negative effect on Dad and me. With you, he has this amazing lust for life. He seems younger, more alive, and I love you for that, you're wonderful. I guess I wanted to call you Mom because of that and because I felt cheated as a child as my mom couldn't be what I wanted—what every kid wanted, for a mother. After I first heard Dad talk about you and then meeting you, I knew you would be the mom I have always dreamed of."

That admission brought more tears from Annie, holding Ned even tighter. After a few minutes, she asked if he would help her lift his dad out of the wheelchair and into the La-Z-Boy so he could get a better night's sleep. Tom was snoring away when they came into the bedroom, but he did wake somewhat, assisting in his extraction from the less-than-comfortable contraption he was wedged in to. Ned gently lifted his father's leg on to the extension, propping it up with some pillows, while Annie covered Tom in the warmest blanket they had; both gave him a kiss, Ned softly telling his dad he loved him and was sorry for yelling at him. They went back to the kitchen and munched a bit on the dinner Annie had prepared earlier, putting the rest in the fridge for tomorrow.

The next morning, Annie and Ned were sipping coffee when a distinct ringing sound came from the bedroom. Annie said she had purchased a small bell for Tom to ring when he was awake and needing to get in his wheelchair or wanting help. Annie told Ned that little noisemaker will disappear when the cast comes off and her man can maneuver on his own.

CHAPTER 32

Ned stayed on another week to make sure his dad was okay and to be confident that Annie could handle all his father's needs. He decided that because he had made an unscheduled trip out because of his dad's accident, he would make arrangements to have his equipment sent out after Christmas as well as his clothes, as he would be staying on after that.

The day of Ned's departure, Annie let Tom and her sweet new son have some private time to talk before they headed to the airport. As Annie was not comfortable leaving Tom at home alone, she had called Brad the day before to see if he or any of his fellow rangers were headed to Kalispell. As it turns out, Brad had a doctor's appointment later in the morning but was happy to pick Ned up early so he could start making his long trek home.

On their way to Glacier Park Airport, Ned asked Brad how Annie did during his father's disappearance. His question caught Brad off guard, and he almost slipped up telling Ned about her attempt at suicide. What he did tell him was that Annie was very brave throughout the ordeal and that she never gave up hope; it was a lie, of course. Ned was grateful for everything he did for his dad and Annie, wondering what he could do to repay him, but Brad waved him off, saying it's something all rangers are taught to do; he was glad it all worked out.

CHAPTER 33

Tom spent much of the day downloading photographs he had taken on his ill-fated trip, to his computer, to be printed out when he was more mobile. Annie went around the house, room to room, coming up with ideas for some decorating. Tom was beautiful, loving, and very caring, but he was no interior decorator; the house most definitely needed some woman's touches. She decided that curtains in the guest rooms would be nice, and the master bedroom could use a valence to define the beautiful window. Fortunately, Tom didn't have a problem with any of that, so Annie started looking through the JC Penney catalog she had ordered, picking out a few styles to show Tom for his approval. While she was at the kitchen table ripping out pages, her cell phone quacked. Looking at the screen showed it was her friend Claire calling.

"Hey, girl, what's up?" Annie asked. "Can't wait for you to come back for Christmas."

"Annie, we had such a great time, and even though Tom was all banged up, I can see why he makes you happy. A real keeper if you ask me. You're a lucky girl. But listen, I have another reason for calling."

Annie was instantly curious by Claire's admission, patiently waiting for the reason her friend had called.

Claire got right to the point. "Terry had a heart attack yesterday and didn't make it. The funeral will be on Friday." Terry was Annie's ex-husband.

For many years, Terry bullied people, even his family, and most of the folks in the little seaside town were afraid of him and what he would do if they ever crossed him. Annie thought she should feel sad, but that emotion never came. Instead, she asked how her daughters were and should she reach out to them.

"Wait on that call, Annie. Right now, the girls are grieving, but in time, I feel confident they will come around. Actually I think that time will be soon."

"What does that mean, Claire? Why the sudden change of heart, what has happened?"

"With Terry gone, people are opening up about what a mean man he was. I spoke with Terry's sister, and she promised me she would tell Kelly and Meghan the truth about their father. I have to believe they will be furious that she hadn't told them before that their father was the abuser and not you, but she was fearful Terry would physically hurt her. He was that mean."

"Oh, Claire, I have prayed for years that my girls would finally hear the truth about their dad. My life would be complete if we were reunited now that I have Tom and Ned in my life."

After hanging up, Annie wept, almost unable to speak, as she processed what Claire had just told her. Tom wheeled over and hugged her as best he could, kissing the back of her neck. After Annie hung up, she and Tom talked about her conversation with Claire and her warning to not get her hopes up. It had been many years since she spoke with her girls, so Claire was right, they may not believe what they were told about their dad. So that she wouldn't stress about hearing or not from her daughters, Annie threw herself back into redecorating the house and taking care of Tom. For the next few days, she measured the windows; and during a trip to the hospital for another checkup for Tom, they stopped at Home Depot and picked up a dozen paint chips so she can decide on the colors in the living room and master bedroom. Annie would have George, the builder, come over with his crew to paint the rooms.

During the visit at the hospital, Tom got good news from the doctor; his leg and arm casts were removed, so he was free of all the plaster he had been wearing for several weeks. He now sported a removable bubble cast on his leg and a padded sling for his left arm. Tom can now get into his own bed and snuggle with his beautiful lady; it had been too many weeks since they had done that.

CHAPTER 34

It's Thanksgiving week, so Annie decided that she and Tom should invite Brad and his wife; Rick, the state trooper who drove her to the hospital; and Brian and his family for a turkey dinner. It would be her way of thanking everyone who helped during and after Tom's accident.

She was thrilled everyone accepted, so she was off to the store to get everything she needed for the feast, and it *would* be a feast to remember. Annie did take a detour to get the turkey as there is a religious group called Hutterites, or Huttes for short. They are farmers and have the best turkeys and organic vegetables you have ever tasted, so Annie ordered a 25 lb. bird and assorted greens that she will pick up the day before.

Turkey Day arrived, and knowing she had a lot of work ahead, Annie had called Abby, a lady in town who did many odd jobs for folks and was also a superb cook. Abby arrived very early and prepared the turkey and vegetables while Annie festively decorated the dining room table and living room. Tom, in his new freedom from plaster and body wrap, gingerly built a nice fire, bringing warmth to the living room. Everything was set for a thankful day, one Annie had thought, weeks prior, would never happen.

Ned called and said he was in Maine with Claire and Betsy. Annie could hear an upbeat tone to his voice, probably because he may have found a lady to spend his life with, like his dad had with her. Ned gave her the revised plan for Christmas and that they will all be arriving on December 18. He also told his father that he had found someone to take over his apartment and that his equipment will be sent out just after Christmas; he was excited about his upcoming move. Annie took the phone back while Tom was limping around whooping his excitement on the great news. She told Ned he can move into her cabin after the girls had gone back to Maine as she wanted everyone under one roof to celebrate the holiday.

Dinner was, as mentioned before, a great feast. Annie said a beautiful prayer that brought tears to all. After pumpkin pie and ice cream, they all retired to the living room and chatted about life and how everyone was grateful for Tom's recovery. Rick was the odd man out but was made to feel as welcome as the others. It turns out he was a widower like Tom and was a year from retirement. Annie figured he was about Claire's age, so the wheels started churning, a possible match for her best friend.

Since Tom was not allowed to drive, as his right leg was still healing and hadn't regained full muscle strength, Annie drove him around town; and with the use of the electric cart, he could help her shop at their grocery store. On the way to the cereal aisle, they stopped at the corner, looked at each other, laughed, and kissed, as that was where they first met; they now call it "Annie and Tom's corner." Off to the drugstore, where Tom had a few dozen photos printed; some would be framed with old barnwood frames he had found at the antique store in town.

CHAPTER 35

The weeks flew by, and it was time to pick up the east coast gang at the airport; Annie drove Tom's car. Needing decorations and a big tree, they left early, stopping at Home Depot, loading up on lights, garland, and other decorations, and then headed to the tent where the trees were all lined up, ready to go to a home to be decorated. The smell was wonderful with all the Fraser and Douglas fir trees, and the choice was hard, but they found a gorgeous eight-foot tree that was full all the way around. After purchasing a fancy holder, they had the tree strapped on top of the SUV and headed to the airport.

Great cheers, hugs, and tears erupted as Claire, Betsy, and Ned came through the security door. All three were pleased to see Tom standing, leaning on a funny-looking cane he had purchased at the antique store in town. It was a special time for Annie to have most everyone, she loved deeply, here for the holiday. The only people missing were her daughters and grandchildren, but she was still happier than she had been for some time. After gathering their luggage, they headed for the car, everyone chatting away. Annie looked over at the "kids" and noticed they were holding hands; wow, how great is that!

The ride home was full of conversation about what had transpired since they were all together and Annie's idea to have everyone help with decorating the house. They all thought that was a great idea.

As Annie pulled into the driveway, her cell phone quacked. Looking at who was calling made her hit the brakes; it was from Kelly, one of her daughters. She told everyone who was calling, so with respect, they all got out and walked to the house, leaving Annie to talk with her girls alone. Tears were welling up as she pressed the button and said hello.

"Mom, it's Kelly and Meghan, we're on a speakerphone. We had to call you as we finally know the truth about what happened years ago. Can you ever forgive us? We're devastated…"

Annie could hear both girls crying; she was crying as well as she told them she held no grudge as they were lied to by their father. She only wished they had learned the truth before now as she had missed them so much. Continuing to speak, Annie said Claire had told her about their father passing away, but she didn't give them any condolences, she couldn't, as he was a horrible man and had hurt her so badly.

"Mom, it's Meghan, we're so sorry, sick about what we just learned. We love you and want to be a part of your life again if you can find it in your heart. We'll understand if you don't."

"Oh, girls, I have prayed this day would come. I never stopped loving you both, and that goes for your children as well. I so much want to see all of you as soon as possible. I have wonderful news to share with you both. First, Claire and Betsy are here for Christmas, and I might as well tell you now: I met the most wonderful man, his name is Tom, and he has an amazing son named Ned."

Annie skipped the details about Tom's accident and her failed attempt at suicide, wanting to keep the conversation positive. She was sobbing now, but they were tears of joy. Her girls kept trying to apologize, but she hushed them each time, saying the past was just that.

Kelly and Meghan were so happy for their mom and were anxious to meet Mr. Wonderful and his son, but in that it was almost Christmas, they couldn't come out to Montana now but would find a time when they can fly out, children and husbands included. They talked for about an hour, Annie having to charge her phone in the dashboard plug, doing their best to catch up for the last six years; but before they ended the call, Annie gave the girls her address and Tom's as well as his cell number, just in case, telling them she loved them both. A promise was made that they would FaceTime with each other on Christmas Day. Annie sat in the car for some time before driving up to the garage and entering the back door. Walking into the living room, she saw everyone on the edge of their seats, anxious to know about the conversation Annie had with her daughters. She looked at all of them and then threw her arms in the air and produced a big smile and a loud whooping noise. Cheers broke out with everyone wanting to know what was said. Once Annie stopped crying, she filled them all in on the conversation and how everything was all right. She also told them that the girls will FaceTime her on Christmas Day, and she wanted to have everyone participate. Tom limped over and gave Annie a huge hug, telling her how happy he was for her. To Annie, her life was now finally complete.

Claire and Annie set off to make dinner while Ned retrieved all the luggage, decorations, and the huge tree, needing some help from Betsy. Tom did his best to hold the tree upright while Ned put the holder on and screwed it tight. Since it was late, the full-scale decorating can wait until tomorrow.

Later, Annie sat on the couch rehashing to herself the conversation she had with her daughters, weeping silently. Tom came over and sat next to her, holding her tight, causing Annie to gasp between tears; she was so happy now. Christmas couldn't come too soon as she desperately wanted to see her daughters and grandchildren on FaceTime; her smile said it all.

CHAPTER 36

It had been a long day for the easterners, so everyone turned in early, each one so happy for Annie. As soon as she and Tom climbed into bed, they engaged in silent but passionate lovemaking; it was as glorious as always.

The next morning, Annie sleepily wandered into the kitchen to find the houseguests preparing a great breakfast. The only person missing was Tom, who limped in a short time later. While sitting around the table, Annie asked who wanted to decorate what in the house. Ned offered to put lights on the bushes and door outside and then help with stringing the tree from the top. They all spent the day making the house festive and ready for the Day. Tom decided no one would be cooking tonight, so he called the Wary Trout and placed an order to be delivered later. He got no argument from anyone as they were all bushed—who said decorating was easy!

For the next two days, Ned and Betsy took off for what they said were day trips; they intentionally didn't include any of the grownups. As a coincidence, Claire, Annie, and Tom started talking about how great it would be if the girls moved out to Hungry Horse or Whitefish. During one of the trips the kids took, Ned and Betsy talked about her coming to live with him, maybe in Whitefish, so when they returned from their last day trip, Betsy brought up her plans of coming out and living with Ned. After the grownups stopped laughing, they explained that they had been talking about the same scenario for Claire and Betsy. Great cheers all around made the day even more exciting. Ned said that he and Betsy had visited the realtor they had found in Whitefish and will start looking at some homes right after Christmas. No one could believe how everything was working out for them, but they were happier for Annie that she will see her daughters soon.

Annie made a few calls and invited the same group they had for Thanksgiving to come over for some holiday cheer on Christmas Eve. Fortunately, Rick, the single guy, was off duty and would be happy to come. On purpose, Annie didn't mention her best friend would be there, nor did she tell Claire about Rick; she didn't want either one to be nervous about the obvious setup. Annie introduced her friends from Maine and Tom's son, making sure Claire knew that Rick was the nice trooper who rushed her to the hospital; Claire told Rick she was grateful for his help. It didn't take her long to do the math to know Annie invited Rick on purpose.

Abby, the town gal who helped at Thanksgiving, came over and made some dishes to nibble on as well as a tasty dessert. With Christmas music playing, everyone gathered around the couch, the young ones sitting on the floor with the puppies, enjoying the fire and the camaraderie. Claire sat next to Rick, smiling while engaged in a quiet conversation; Annie definitely felt like a matchmaker. Everyone had a place to sit except Tom, so he went into the bedroom and came out wielding his wheelchair, which made everyone laugh. Annie thought, *Now that Tom is mobile, that contraption will be returning to the medical rental company right after Christmas.*

As it was getting late, all the guests headed home to wait for Santa to arrive, bidding the hosts and houseguests a good night and a Merry Christmas; promises were made for another gathering on New Year's Eve. Rick was the last to leave, hanging around as the others drove away. Claire walked out with him and chatted for a while before she ran back in as it was bitter cold outside. With a sheepish look on her face, she gave Annie a big smile and a thankful wink for inviting Rick. Apparently, they made plans for a date the day after Christmas; Annie, of course, was thrilled.

CHAPTER 37

Christmas Day was joyous; all the gifts were either useful or appreciated. It was by far the nicest Christmas Annie had had for a long time.

After a wonderful midday lunch cooked by Abby, they all bundled up and went for only a short walk as Mr. Gimpy was still a bit unsteady.

Just as they walked into the house, Annie's cell phone quacked; it was a FaceTime from her girls.

"Merry Christmas, my darling daughters," Annie said as she once again started to cry seeing her girls for the first time in six years. "You both look so beautiful. I can't believe my eyes. How was your Christmas, where are the kids?" All three grandchildren appeared and waved hi, seemingly a bit curious about who was the woman they were looking at. Annie walked over and stretched her arm straight out so her girls could see Tom and Ned. All were excited to meet each other even though it was by phone. Meghan piped up asking her mother how in the world she could have hooked such a gorgeous man, laughing as she said it. There was a lot of catching-up between the girls, but before they hung up, Kelly and Meghan asked when they could come out. Plans were made that sometime in May or June would be best for them as the kids will be out of school. Many kisses and words of love were given with promises to call soon.

"Annie, your girls are beautiful," Tom said, "just like their mother. I can't imagine how happy you are right now, you deserve it. I'm looking forward to meeting them all soon."

Annie was speechless, smiling through tears. She never thought the day would come that she would be reunited with her girls. Spring couldn't come too soon, but it will be great to be able to call them and talk whenever she wanted.

The next day was spent making a game plan for the new year. Ned's clothes and personal items were on their way along with his equipment, so he could continue producing software for his company back in New York. Claire would head home, putting the house on the market but would come out in the spring regardless of whether the house had sold or not; Claire's wonderful husband had left her well-off financially before he died. Betsy decided to stay and be with Ned, asking her mom to pack up her clothes and send them out as soon as she got home. A trip to Whitefish for some winter clothes would be necessary before her wardrobe showed up.

It was time for Claire to get ready for her date with Rick, so she headed to her room to prepare for her first evening with a man in over ten years; she was nervous for sure. Ned and Betsy took off with the dogs for a short walk, leaving Annie and Tom alone by the fire.

Tom spoke first.

"Annie, I love you so much, you are the brightest star in the sky, I couldn't be happier. At our age, a long engagement is silly, so now that I'm back to almost being myself and that you have connected with your girls, I think it's time we set a date. Is there a day that would be special for you?"

Annie's face lit up, challenging the brightness of the Christmas tree lights behind her. For her, there were many special days; in fact, every day was special being with this incredible man, but she wanted to choose the *most* important day, and that, to her, was when she crashed her grocery cart with Tom's. Annie pulled out a calendar she had gotten for Christmas and saw that March 12, the day they met, was a Friday. Tom agreed that that was the most important date in their lives so far, so breaking from a traditional Saturday for most weddings, it was settled. The kids and Claire came into the living room, curious as to why Annie was in Tom's lap, hugging and kissing him; she had a huge smile from ear to ear.

Cheers broke out, more hugs, as Annie and Tom told them their plans and the date they chose. Claire said she would now come out sooner to help Annie plan her wedding; Betsy said she would help as well. Rick arrived and, after hearing the news, was thrilled, promising to make sure he had that day off. Claire and Rick then took off to the Wary Trout for what she hoped would be a fun and romantic dinner; no doubt it will. Annie called her daughters back and gave them the great news; their travel plans would change as they wanted to celebrate the day with their mom and Tom, their soon-to-be new dad. Besides, they will be bridesmaids in the wedding.

CHAPTER 38

Over the next few days, the gang did some exploring, even taking a ride up to the top of the ski slope on the chairlifts to have lunch at the Hell Roaring Café. It was a chilly round trip for sure, but the view was exhilarating; everyone had a blast. The Christmas group all came over New Year's Eve for another fun evening; everyone was happy about the upcoming nuptials.

Betsy and Ned took Claire to the airport two days later and then perused around Kalispell, window-shopping and going to two furniture stores looking for their future home needs. When they arrived back, they packed their clothes and headed over to Annie's house, the kids' new home for a few months. Before they left, Annie showed Ned and Betsy how to use the bear spray just in case, making sure they carried it whenever they were outside; to say Betsy had a worried look on her face was an understatement. It was January, so the bears were still in hibernation, but you just never know.

Tom and Annie were finally alone, but they weren't complaining as they loved having the house full of people, but they were in need of some quiet time. Annie went back to hanging the curtains she bought, and Tom helped George, as best he could, with painting, something that wasn't too stressful on his healing body. The kids did come over the next night for dinner, having stopped by the Outback Steakhouse in Columbia Falls, picking up a smorgasbord of food, so they all munched and talked until late. Both couples marveled at their new relationships and how a near tragedy had brought Betsy and Ned together. Later, after the kids went home, while lying in bed wrapped in Tom's arms, Annie spoke about the incredible ten months since they met.

"Darling man, before I met you, my life was lonely. Oh, I had friends, just friends, but I really wanted to have someone special to share my life with. With no eligible man in town, I had resigned myself to just go through life alone, and then we crashed our shopping carts, and everything changed. I pinch myself every day to make sure I'm not dreaming. Thankfully you're still here. My joy is unmeasurable, and I only hope I have given you as much happiness as you have given me." She passionately kissed his chest, lightly squeezing his now healed ribs.

"Annie," Tom chimed in, "you have brought a new life into my lonely soul. I never thought I would ever love again, especially to someone so amazing as you. Every day with you is a dream come true. I can't wait to see what the next day brings us and all the days after that. I wish our special day was today. How would you like to go to the justice of the peace to be legally married now, or wait until March for the formal wedding?"

"Oh, Tom, I think to marry you sooner sounds wonderful. I don't want you changing your mind." A small laugh emanated from her lips. "Maybe we can go to the courthouse in Kalispell tomorrow and celebrate later at the Wary Trout." They continued to hold each other, quietly kissing until they both fell asleep.

CHAPTER 39

Snow was falling heavily as they rose the next morning. The forecast was for five to six inches with more snow tomorrow; their trip to the courthouse would be postponed—no worries, as they have plenty of time. Tom called George, the builder.

"Thank you for the threshold that gave me access to the house when I was wheelchair bound, but could you remove it? And while at the house, can we talk about adding a small office off the kitchen? And oh, by the way, do you know anyone who plows driveways?" As it turned out, George did plow in the winter when business was slow, so he would come over tomorrow to clear Tom's road and then sit down and draw up some plans for the addition to be built in the spring after the snow was gone.

Last November, Tom had purchased a large shed to house his tools and for the wood, so he went out to bring in a couple of armfuls for the bread oven and fireplace. On the second run, Tom rushed back in the house calling for Annie to hurry outside. Panicked that something had happened to her man, Annie ran through the house and out to the shed. Tom was standing there looking out to the field in the back, and there stood a huge moose munching on whatever grass wasn't covered by the falling snow. Tom dashed into the house and grabbed his camera, quickly snapping off over a dozen photos of the magnificent beast. At one point, the moose turned and looked at the two humans, nodding his head up and down as if he was saying hi; eventually he strolled off into the woods.

"That was amazing," Tom said. "What a beautiful animal. I hope he comes back. I've read they can be dangerous, so I'm glad I have a telephoto lens."

Annie, having lived here longer than Tom, had seen several moose, but as she told him, "It's always exciting to see one. They are majestic." After bringing in a good supply of wood, the two of them continued the decorating of the house, which, when done, brought a smile to Tom's face; he loved it all.

With nowhere to go today, the two lovebirds decided to play some card games before they fixed dinner. Later while lying on the couch, Annie remarked that she would like a couch like hers at the cabin where the two of them could lie side by side without fear of falling off, so when they do get to Kalispell next, they can stop at the huge furniture store and pick out one suitable to their romantic needs; Tom had a brilliant idea to donate his couch to Ned and Betsy.

CHAPTER 40

It was only lightly snowing the next morning, so Tom called George and asked him to go over to Annie's place and plow out the kids' driveway before he comes over to his house. Tom then called Ned to tell him about George's arrival and the idea of tying the knot and would they like to be witnesses. He also asked Ned if he and Betsy would like the couch in the living room. He got a yes on both counts; Ned was excited about being a witness to his father's preformal wedding idea.

After both driveways were cleared, the kids drove over to Tom's house, and they all took off to Kalispell after Tom and George made some plans for the office; the snow had tapered off to flurries.

The informal marriage took about ten minutes after filling out a few forms, and then they drove over to Wrights Furniture store to try out a few couches. With so many to choose from, Annie and Tom thought it would be fun to "test-drive" a few, lying down on them and snuggling. The salesman was amused, but Betsy and Ned were embarrassed, so they wandered off to look for some pieces for their future home. Great cheers could be heard throughout the store as the newlyweds found the perfect couch; they were like two kids in a toy store to say the least.

Having made their purchase and making arrangements for a delivery tomorrow, they went to have lunch at a Mongolian restaurant in town called Hu Hot. While waiting for their meals to arrive, Betsy spoke.

"Tom, you know I love Annie, she's my second mom. Now that Ned is calling her Mom, can I call you Dad? My father was a wonderful man, but so are you, so I hope you say yes, it would make me very happy."

"Betsy," Tom said, "nothing would make me happier to have a daughter like you. I knew when we first met that someday you would be a part of our family, so yes, I would be honored for you to call me Dad." Hugs and kisses followed.

CHAPTER 41

It had been a long day when they got back to Hungry Horse, but Ned and Betsy took off to Whitefish to enjoy the nightlife on Central Avenue, and the two "old folks" raided the fridge, plopping themselves on the couch in front of the fire. Because the new lounging piece of furniture arrives tomorrow, they both felt it fitting that after they finished eating, they would once again go prone for the last time, wrapping themselves in each other's arms under a cozy blanket.

Tom looked at Annie and said, "Welcome to the family, Mrs. McGuire," kissing her passionately before they fell asleep.

Annie called Claire in the morning telling her about what transpired the day before at the courthouse, and of course Claire was thrilled. She was also happy to know that Betsy had asked Tom about calling him Dad, as Betsy had called her recently to see if she thought that would be okay; Betsy can also call Annie *Mom*, if she liked. Claire told Annie she will be coming out in a couple of weeks and will stay at her cabin until after the wedding, hopefully finding a house to buy in town. She also filled her in on her budding relationship with Rick, saying they have spoken every night since she got back to Maine. It must be something in the air that there was so much love flying around. It looked like Claire, and Rick might be getting serious. To the newlyweds' delight, the new couch arrived and was placed in front of the fireplace; they would try it out tonight.

CHAPTER 42

Weeks sailed by. Claire arrived and decided to stay at Tom and Annie's instead until the "kids" found a house to buy but will move to the cabin when Annie's girls and family arrived for the wedding. Annie has spoken several times a week with her girls and grandchildren, keeping them up to date with the goings-on, also wanting to know how everything was back east. What a joy it was to have the newest technology that enables people to see each other on the phone. The grandkids were beautiful and seemingly less shy each time they saw their grandmother. Since the little ones were only prefirst or first grade, taking them out of school to fly out for the wedding would be okay; they won't miss much.

Claire and Annie went to a dress shop in Whitefish and picked out a beautiful western dress that was appropriate for a second marriage. The guys decided to wear navy blazers, open white dress shirts with a turtleneck underneath, blue jeans with hiking boots; this is Montana, so nothing fancy for the big day. While in Whitefish, Annie bought the puppies some bright new collars and colorful winter dog jackets as they will be part of the ceremony. Claire found some nice invitations, so when they got home, both she and Annie began to address them to the small invited group. While the girls were shopping, Tom, Betsy, and Ned scoped out a few places to have the wedding and, with permission from Annie, chose a spot at the end of Lake MacDonald with a gorgeous view of Glacier Park. More than likely, there will be snow on the ground, so Tom found a guy, who happened to live in West Glacier, to plow an area for the ceremony. Tom also went to the local rental store and ordered stand-up gas heaters delivered just in case it was too cold.

Kelly and Meghan called and told their mom about their new travel plans; they will stay a week or more—no argument from Annie. For the rest of the day, Annie felt as if she was floating around the house, excited about seeing her girls and grandchildren. Tom, at one point, started to laugh as Annie had checked both guest rooms several times to make sure everything was perfect. Claire decided, instead, to move over to Rick's cabin while Annie's family was here; Betsy and Ned were thrilled with Claire's decision as their privacy would not be disrupted a bit.

It was decided to have the reception at Tom's house, so Claire took on the chore of overseeing the event. She found a wonderful catering company in Whitefish called Artichoke, and had the owner come out to the house and go over the menu and logistics. There was a nice bakery associated with the grocery store in town, so Claire stopped by to design the cake. Everything was in place for the big day; now it was time to relax and enjoy some quiet moments before her girls and children arrive and pandemonium breaks out. To make sure the little ones were comfortable, Annie bought a tent big enough for three and sleeping bags to be erected in the living room; they should get a kick out of that.

CHAPTER 43

The big day was in less than a week away. The girls and family were arriving in two days, and all Annie can do was dance around with a huge smile on her face. As happy as she was, Annie was also nervous about seeing her girls. It had been six years since she physically saw them last, and it wasn't a happy time; she prayed every day their first greeting would be a joyous one. Because there would be seven people flying in, Tom arranged to rent a small passenger van as the two cars they have wouldn't accommodate everyone; fortunately, he had been cleared last week by his doctor to drive.

The night before, Annie hardly slept a wink. Instead she wrapped herself around Tom, holding him tight, trembling from excitement, finally dozing off to have some sweet dreams.

The next day, Tom and Annie left a bit early for the airport as the van was in another location across town. After signing all the forms, they drove both vehicles to the airport, parked in short term, and went inside. To add to the drama, the plane was going to be twenty minutes late, so Annie and Tom got coffee and a sticky bun to bide the time. All Tom could do was smile looking at his beautiful lady's face, tears rolling down her cheeks. Reaching over and taking her hands, Tom reassured Annie that everything will be fine.

The announcement finally came that Flight 464 from Chicago had landed; soon her girls will be coming through the security door and be reunited with their mother. It took another agonizing fifteen minutes before folks began coming out to the main terminal; Annie stretched as tall as she could to see over the arriving passengers. Finally, Kelly and Meghan came out, followed by their husbands and children. Spotting their mother, they both ran over, each grabbing their mom, holding her tight. All three girls were crying hysterically, not saying a word. Passengers who strolled by were smiling as they knew this must be a happy moment. Tom walked over and greeted the girls' husbands, Tony and John, and the little ones, Jack, Isabel, and Sam. It was some time before the girls separated, and then they just looked at each other, crying and smiling at the same time.

"Oh, Mom," Kelly said, "you look even more beautiful than the last time we saw you."

Meghan piped in that her mom also looked younger. They hugged again before going over so Annie could meet the grandkids and their dads. Needless to say, the girls were thrilled to meet Tom, each giving him a hug and a kiss while Annie knelt down to say hi to the little ones. If Annie had been nervous before, her grandchildren gathered around and hugged their Gammy, the name they chose to call their grandmother, making her feel loved; Tony and John both hugged the mother-in-law they had never met. More tears and kisses followed until it was time to head home. Annie drove the SUV with the girls while Tom loaded up all the kids and their fathers in the van for the ride to Hungry Horse.

Annie called Claire and told them they were on the way and mentioned that all went well at the airport. An hour later, Claire, Betsy, and Ned greeted the two vehicles as they drove up to the house, helping to bring in the luggage. The girls gave Claire and Betsy big hugs, and after the introductions, Ned got some as well.

It was early evening before everyone was settled, so Tom called the Wary Trout and had dinner brought over; no one was cooking tonight. Before the families flew out, Annie, during one of their many calls, made the girls promise not to apologize about what happened many years ago. This would be a happy reunion followed by a beautiful wedding at the lake. At one point, both girls and Annie went off to have a chat by themselves, Kelly and Meghan telling their mom how much they loved her and, oh by the way, Tom was gorgeous.

Tom built one of his great fires, so they all gathered in the living room, everyone wanting to get a word in. Annie had bought the kids some toys and a train set, and they were also having fun playing and tussling with the puppies before they crashed for the night; it had been a long day. Annie helped her daughters get the little ones settled in the tent, giving each a nice hug and a kiss. Tom and Ned got to know Tony and John better before the girls returned, and then they bid each other a good night with a promise to see everyone in the morning. Betsy and Ned dropped Claire off at Rick's place and then headed over to the cabin.

The next day was a gorgeous warm day, unlike most days at the beginning of March. The kids from the cabin came over early, letting the dogs out, and began to fix a good old-fashioned Montana breakfast for all the easterners. Annie shuffled in followed by Meghan and Kelly, all helping themselves to a big mug of coffee. Claire and Rick arrived just in time to enjoy a hearty meal. The rest of the troops came in with Tom soon poking his head in the kitchen, which was now overflowing. Since the wedding was a few days away, the discussion turned to what to do. Tony needed to make a few calls to his law firm, and John wanted to check in at the hardware store he owned to make sure all was going well in his absence; the little ones found their way back to the toys and train.

CHAPTER 44

Annie thought it would be fun to go to Whitefish for some shopping and lunch with all the girls; the guys and children were content to stay put in town for the day with the suggestion they go to the Glacier Inn for lunch and tour the area ending up at Annie's cabin so they could see where he and Ned learned to fly-fish. With caution, the kids wandered over to the river after Ned had shoveled a narrow path; kids love water. When they get a little older, Gammy can teach them how to catch that elusive trout.

Both John and Tony were very impressed with what they saw, so when the two were alone, they talked about coming out to live in northwest Montana someday; life in their seaside town in Maine apparently wasn't very exciting, so before the kids get older, it might a good time to head west. Tony grabbed a phone book and looked up law firms in the yellow pages, finding two large ones in Whitefish that did many types of law. He called them both, setting up appointments for the next day. John also looked up hardware stores and found one called WBC in Whitefish that happened to be hiring. Knowing that his longtime manager back home would buy his store, he decided to speak with Meghan to see what she thought; Tony did the same with Kelly.

At first the girls were taken aback but, after giving it some thought, decided that moving out west would be great, especially for the kids. That night at dinner, Annie's girls announced that both families wanted to move out to Whitefish to be close to their mom, if that was okay with her. At that admission, Annie totally lost it, weeping tears of joy. What a whirlwind time it has been since she and Tom met, with Claire deciding to move to the area and Betsy and Tom's son, Ned, becoming a serious couple. And now to have her girls and grandkids move out soon with their husbands—it just seemed so surreal.

CHAPTER 45

The big day finally arrived. There was a crystal-clear sky albeit a tad chilly, but no one seemed to mind. The area by the lake had been cleared, heaters delivered, and the small group of invited guests gathered to witness the happiest day in Annie's and Tom's lives. Reverend McAllister, the Episcopal priest in town, stood with his back to the lake as Tom, Ned, Brian, and Rick, along with Barley, waited for Annie to take the short walk down to a beautifully decorated gazebo. Claire, Betsy, Meghan, and Kelly with grandkids came down first with Cooper, the dog, in front of Annie, who was escorted by Brad; Cooper was carrying a small box affixed to his collar, which had the rings inside. Of course, this adorable golden retriever had to stop and say hello to everyone in attendance, making the guests laugh, so it took a while for Annie to reach her wonderful man and take his hand. After Father McAllister said his opening lines, Kelly and Meghan, along with Ned, read passages from the Bible; and then it was Annie's and Tom's turns to say their vows, bringing everyone to tears.

The heaters did their job, but it was still cold, so after the pronouncement and kiss, everyone headed back to Tom and Annie's for the reception.

Once back at the house, Abby, along with the catering company, brought out several yummy delights for everyone to enjoy along with champagne to celebrate with the newlyweds. After cake was served, Annie thought she should explain to everyone why the wedding was on this date and not some time during the summer when it was warmer. Everyone cheered after they heard about the crashing carts, and all felt it was apropos.

The day was winding down, and several of the guests departed, giving best wishes to the bride and groom. Rick stuck around—looks like there might be another wedding in the air; so all who were left, mostly family, gathered around the fireplace and talked about the day and how excited they all were for Tom and Annie.

CHAPTER 46

The girls and their families stuck around for a few more days, taking trips into Whitefish to scope out the town and for the guys to find work. Both John and Tony did secure jobs, so Kelly and Meghan went to see Ned's realtor, Mitzie, giving her their desired needs. Hopefully she can find them homes before the fall, when the little ones would be going to school in town. Annie and Tom decided to delay their honeymoon until later in the summer so if Mitzie found some homes, Annie could go take a look and report back to her girls. Also, Tom wanted to go back to the British Isles in early fall to show Annie other areas where his family came from; that time of year was the best time, weather-wise, to visit.

Not wanting to stretch their resources too thin, Ned and Betsy found a very cute condo overlooking Whitefish Lake, so once the paper work and financing is finalized, they will move out of Annie's cabin, so Claire can settle in by herself with a more than an occasional visit from Rick. Time will tell, but it looked like there could be two weddings coming soon; the joy in everyone's life couldn't be measured.

Tom and Annie have spoken often about what the future looks like, and because Tom had retired quite comfortably, financially speaking, they decided to take several trips a year out of the country. Neither one had been to Hawaii or New Zealand, so they visited the Flathead Travel Agency to gather brochures for some trips next year. Tom also decided that he didn't want Annie doing housework, so he hired Abby to come over three days a week, and when they do travel, she can puppy-sit. Abby was thrilled as the small jobs she does in town didn't quite pay all the bills.

Claire came over several times a week, bringing Rick, when he's not on patrol; each time they looked closer to announcing their future intentions. Claire got the word that a nice couple from Portland have decided to buy her house, wanting a quick closing in three weeks. With that, she made arrangements to fly home and pack up the furnishings—leaving, no doubt, a lot to the local charities she has supported over the years. Rick has some vacation time saved up, so he decided to go with Claire and help with the move; as Annie suspected, they were now officially a serious couple.

When it turns out that Rick and Claire make a commitment of marriage, Rick's cabin, which he bought with his widow many years ago, was quite adequate for Claire; she won't have to buy a house. The cabin was decorated beautifully, so if she were to move in, Rick would probably be okay with changing a few things around to make it feel like it is her home now.

With Rick going with her mom back east, Betsy made a list of some personal items she wanted along with all her clothes and a few pieces of furniture. Ned's equipment had arrived in early January, so he was busy setting up all the tools of his trade in the house to begin working on some new software the company asked for. Betsy did find a job at the Toggery, a very Western clothing and boot shop on Central Avenue; she'll start next week.

CHAPTER 47

With some much-needed quiet time, Tom and Annie decided to kick back and do as little as possible for a few days. With a short trip to the grocery store, using one cart, they replenished all the necessities, including the fridge and freezer, and then headed to Whitefish to stock up on dog food, bringing the four-legged wonders with them. Ned called wanting to know if they wanted to do lunch, but Tom declined, choosing instead to spend the day alone with Annie. With a wonderful lunch at the Tupelo Grill, the two lovebirds found themselves staring at each other, both smiling at their good fortune. They talked about how they first met, admitting that they felt their lives were destined to be singular. But fate has a way of appearing in strange ways, like the crashing of the grocery carts, Tom's disappearance bringing her best friend and goddaughter out, and the budding romances of Betsy and Ned and Claire and Rick, only to be topped by Annie and her daughters being reunited. To say the last several months have been like a fairy-tale adventure is an understatement.

Returning to Hungry Horse, Annie brought up the idea of selling her cabin, but Tom squelched that idea thinking that she should rent it out during the summer months to fishermen coming to the area. Since the cabin was paid for, and he has plenty in the bank, it would give Annie some money of her own. Besides, it was their favorite fishing spot where Tom learned how to catch that elusive trout, so there was some sentimentality involved. The thought was that Brian, the fly shop owner, could add the rental to his website and post it in his shop, hopefully filling the cabin for several months in the summer and fall.

CHAPTER 48

With wonderful farmers markets in West Glacier, Columbia Falls, and Whitefish, Annie spoke with Tom about expanding her herb and flower garden at her cabin so she could sell those items at the markets during the summer. Tom thought it was a great idea, so off they went to Home Depot to purchase wire, fencing material, black gold soil, and of course, more seeds and bulbs. As soon as the snow was gone, and the existing garden has firmed up, Tom will rent a rototiller to prepare the ground for planting.

Tom got a call from Brad at the park wondering if he wanted to come back this summer to do more talks and hikes to the tourists, adding one on the perils of solo hiking. The park won't open for a couple of months, but Tom felt certain he would be there. He could use that time to do some reading so he will be prepared for some fun treks along the many trails, giving the tourists an experience to remember.

Claire called Annie telling her that they would be returning next week having hired a moving company, tagging everything to come out and, with Rick's help, putting aside many items for charity. She said Rick has been wonderful, and they have enjoyed having the time together. Claire thanked Annie for introducing her to Rick as he is so loving and caring that she can't wait to spend her life with him. She told Annie that she will move out of the cabin shortly after returning and move in with Rick.

The next morning, as she had done several times before, Annie woke early and moved to the end of the bed, staring out the window. She thought back to the day she left Maine and moved out to Hungry Horse, leaving her girls behind. It was the saddest day of her life, one that has haunted her for years. Then came the day she met

Tom, and in an instant, her life changed. Through quiet tears she smiled thinking about the day they crashed their carts at the grocery store, their first date, and the other wonderful times that they had spent together. Annie also reflected on the day Tom didn't come home from his hike and the despair she felt thinking that he wasn't coming back, and then he was found badly injured but alive. Annie also thought about Claire and Betsy and meeting Tom's son, who now calls her *Mom*. Having her girls and grands in her life now has capped off an amazing time. All these emotions made her sob quietly, waking Tom from his slumber. Moving behind her, he wrapped his arms around his new bride, holding her tight, understanding why she was crying. Tom's eyes became a bit moist as well as he told her how much she means to him and how he looks forward to the next day that he can spend with her.

CHAPTER 49

The fairy tale continued as Ned and Betsy were now engaged, no formal date set. Claire and Rick decided that at their age, they were happy just living together, but that could change. Annie's girls and family moved out in late August, having bought homes next to each other in a new development just south of Whitefish; the kids will be starting school soon.

Tom has enjoyed giving lectures to the many tourists that came to Glacier Park, and Annie has picked up a few more hours at the fly shop as Brian had two floats a day with fishermen. In that this area is dog friendly, Brian told Annie she could bring the puppies to work, and they have instantly become celebrities with all who came in to purchase their fishing needs. When she wasn't at the shop, she and the dogs drove over to spend time with her daughters and kids, catching up after so many years apart. For Annie, to say her life was perfect now would be an understatement. She couldn't have scripted it any better, and it all began when she crashed into Tom with her shopping cart—an unusual way to begin an amazing romance.

CHAPTER 50

The summer slipped by without any issues until late September, when a lightning storm struck in the park, starting a forest fire west of Lake MacDonald. It had been a dry summer, so the forest was ripe for a major burn. Crews from the surrounding states and Canada were called to hopefully extinguish the fire before it got out of control. Brad summoned all his rangers and gave everyone an assignment just in case the major part of the park was affected like it was a few years back.

In the fire's path was a turn-of-the-twentieth-century log village called Kelly Camp. Every effort was made to keep the flames from reaching this old lakeside compound, but the breadth of the fire was massive, burning each cabin to the ground. So far, the fire had not yet jumped the lake, so the park was still open to tourists. Daily reports were circulated, keeping the rangers informed as to the fires progress, and eventually the west side of the park along the Going to the Sun Road had to be cut off, and a road block at Logan Pass was erected, keeping the tourists from coming in from the east entrance to the park, heading further west as the smoke was too thick for good visibility along the narrow road.

Annie decided to form a volunteer group to help give some respite to the weary firefighters. She went to the grocery stores in the area asking for food and water donations. She then organized a group to bring these brave folks over to the house, where she and the others cooked meals, also letting the fire fighters use her cabin for showers and a bed. Tom did his part to keep an eye out for any fires that may crop up from sparks drifting over the lake, as did the other rangers stationed throughout the two million acres of the park. This meant hiking certain trails but with another ranger; no solos allowed for anyone, especially Tom.

The massive fire raged on for almost a month before a weeklong rain doused the area, helping the crews get it under control. The days following the storm were spent clearing charred areas and putting out smoldering brush and trees.

During the tragedy in the park, Annie and Tom didn't get to spend much time together, both busy doing their part to help save the park. On most evenings, Tom and the other rangers were still making sure everything was under control. When the newlyweds were able to be alone, they made the best of it; making love was never sacrificed because of exhaustion.

CHAPTER 51

Life soon returned to normal for Annie and Tom; the fire was finally under control. They had each other, and all their children now lived nearby; they were still very much in love. Even the puppies were having fun entertaining everyone they met at the fly shop or in town. Ned and Betsy were loving life in Whitefish, and Claire and Rick have fallen even deeper in love. As for Annie's girls and families, their new lives in northwest Montana were exciting. The kids, along with their fathers, were learning to fly-fish with Annie's help, and Kelly and Meghan were enjoying being involved with the kids' school.

This winter, all seven easterners will take up skiing. If there was a portrait of the million-dollar family, all the characters in Annie's life would be in the picture.

Great news from the lovebirds in Whitefish; they were expecting a child in eight months. Like Tom and Annie, they went to the courthouse to be legally married and will have a small wedding later. Tom, having not been a grandfather before, was super-excited about the upcoming birth. He was already planning fun things to do with the child even though it will be a few years before the little one is even walking. Occasionally, it was decided, Annie will get to babysit for her grands when her girls and husbands take an adult vacation or a night out; they will never get an argument from their mother as she adored the three munchkins. "Anytime," was what she tells her girls.

CHAPTER 52

One thing Tom and Annie thought to be a good idea was to once a month have a wish list conversation. With both being busy, it was thought that they needed to make sure they were both happy and to discuss any wants and needs that require a mutual agreement. Tom thought having a few horses on the property would be fun, and besides, it would bring all the families together more often—Claire and Rick included, of course. Annie knew of a breeder in Coram, Henry Conner, and Tom found a barn builder in East Glacier, so he gave the guy, Tucker Wilson, a call and had him come over to discuss the location and size of the barn. It was decided that a four-stall barn would be a great start, making sure an addition could be added later; construction will begin soon before winter set in. Next, Tom and Annie drove over to the horse farm and picked out four beautiful horses to be delivered once the barn was complete. Henry told them they could come over anytime and help take care of all seventeen horses he has—that way they both can learn the ropes, as it were, prior to their horses coming to their new home.

It took almost a month to complete the barn, and a good size paddock was built in Tom's field behind the house; so a week before Thanksgiving, Henry brought the new members of the family over to great shouts and applause by all the families. Henry also brought over a large supply of hay and straw, showing everyone, little ones included, how to spread the yellow stuff. Tom and Tony had previously been to Whitefish to purchase saddles and harnesses, and John was able to buy horse feed from the hardware store where he worked, getting a nice discount. The plan was for the kids, all sizes, to ride around the paddock and for the adults to walk the horses through the woods. Tom surveyed the new construction, concluding that since everyone loved the horses, an additional four stalls would be built once winter was over.

CHAPTER 53

Thanksgiving arrived, and like last year, the meal was outstanding; it was the first major one with everyone together. Abby outdid herself with the main meal and homemade pumpkin pie for dessert. Since she has been working for Annie and Tom for a while now, and being a lovely person to boot, everyone decided that she should be considered part of the family and join them at the dinner table. Tears welled up as she has been a widow for some time and her adult kids lived far away, not seeing their mother very often; she was grateful for the "adoption." Betsy asked Abby if she would help her once the baby was born when her mom would not be available, and of course, she said yes.

Speaking of Claire, she is working part-time as a barista at the Craggy Moose; and in two months, Rick will retire from the state police and join Tom working as a part-time ranger in the park. Claire and Rick have decided to get married at an early June wedding; now, Annie really felt like a matchmaker. If you had been thinking that someone should make a movie out of the recent adventures, you would be correct. Whoever said life has many twists and turns was right.

On the road of life, it's not where you go but who
you spend it with that makes all the difference.

The end

Lost and Found is a story of love, tragedy, and family.

The inspiration for the story came from living in a beautiful part of the country, Northwest Montana and Glacier Park.

ABOUT THE AUTHOR

Cooke Boyd grew up on the east coast, but after several visits to Northwest Montana, a permanent move to the area took place several years ago. Inspired by the beauty of the area and with imagination, Boyd's first book, *Life in Montana*, was what he envisioned what life would have been like having lived in Montana all his life.

CPSIA information can be obtained
at www.ICGtesting.com
Printed in the USA
BVHW021700220223
658708BV00005B/44